And the evening and the morning were the fourth day.
And God said, Let the waters bring forth abundantly the moving creature that hath life, and fowl that may fly above the earth in the open firmament of heaven.
And God c
great whale
living creature that
waters brought forth abundantly, after their kind, and every winged fowl after his kind: and God saw that it was good.
And God blessed them, saying, Be fruitful and multiply, and fill the waters in the seas, and let fowl multiply in the earth. And the evening and the morning were the fifth day.
And God said, Let the earth bring forth the living creature after his kind, cattle and creeping thing, and beast of the earth after his kind: and it was so.
And God made the beast of the earth after his kind
And God saw that it was good.
And God said, Let us make man in our image, after our likeness: and let them have dominion over fish of the sea, and over the fowl of the air, and over the cattle, and over all the earth, and over every creeping thing that creepeth upon the earth.
And God created man in his own image, in the image of God created he him; male and female created he them. And God blessed them, and God said unto them, Be fruitful and multiply, and replenish the earth, and subdue it: and have dominion over the fish of the sea, and over the fowl of the air, and over every living thing that moveth upon the earth.
And God saw everything that he had made, and, behold, it was very good.
R.K.

World-Famous

PAINTINGS

GIOVANNI BELLINI · BOTTICELLI · LEONARDO DA
VINCI · ALBERTINELLI · MICHELANGELO · TITIAN
RAPHAEL · ANDREA DEL SARTO · CORREGGIO
BORDONE · MORONI · JAN VAN EYCK · MEMLING
MABUSE · RUBENS · VAN DYCK · DÜRER · HOL-
BEIN · FRANS HALS · REMBRANDT · TER BORCH
DE HOOCH · METSU · VERMEER · MAES · HOBBE-
MA · VELASQUEZ · MURILLO · WATTEAU · NAT-
TIER · CHARDIN · BOUCHER · PERRONEAU
GREUZE · FRAGONARD · LE BRUN · MILLET
COROT · MEISSONIER · MUENIER · VAN GOGH
CÉZANNE · RENOIR · MANET · HOGARTH · REYN-
OLDS · GAINSBOROUGH · ROMNEY · RAEBURN
MORLAND · LAWRENCE · TURNER · CONSTABLE
COX · DE WINT · MACLISE · WATTS · BROWN
LANDSEER · ROSSETTI · MILLAIS · BURNE-JONES
YEAMES · ORCHARDSON · PETTIE · HOLIDAY
MOORE · SOMERSCALES · PARSONS · COTMAN
WHISTLER · HOMER · EAKINS · MILLET · RYDER
SARGENT · BELLOWS · WOOD

WISE & CO., INC., NEW YORK

World - Famous

PAINTINGS

*

Edited by

ROCKWELL KENT

*

WISE & CO., INC., NEW YORK

Pictures and Painters

→»*«←

Introduction

※*※

A MASTER with whom I studied used to say to us: "The more
fragile and delicate the subject of your picture the stronger
and bolder must be your manner of painting it." The corollary
of such counsel invites us to reflect that the more solemn the subject of discussion the more gayly, perhaps, must it be handled; and
to suspect that life at its utmost may be just like that: all opposites.
Weak men are cruel; strong men, kind. And a proverb of William
Blake reminds us (as though we could ever forget it!) that "Excess
of sorrow laughs. Excess of joy weeps."

Certainly Art, the subject and the matter of this volume—being
of itself the enshrinement of men's most devout and reverent
moods—is of an order of creation essentially solemn enough to
deserve of all things just such light-hearted and gay discussion as
may best dispose our minds to its full enjoyment.

Solemn? We'll say it is! Don't they house it for our enjoyment (!)
in the most frigid and cheerless of marble halls, submitting us
to such tortures of foot weariness as no one but a penitential pilgrim should endure? Do they not deprive us pilgrims to Art's
shrines of the solace of a smoke, of the relief of speaking above a
whisper, of the good cheer of a friendly bar? Don't they count us
through clinking turnstiles as we go in, search us with Roentgen
eyes as we go out; and watch us in between like Hoover G-men on
the trail of spies? We to whom the mere aspect of a Park Avenue
doorman strikes terror, in what a mood for Art—how far from
carefree, happy, at our ease are we when, passing through the safe-
deposit portals of Art's shrines, their death-like penitentiary mood
enfolds us! Stop! No more of this. Art being solemn, we'll enliven
it. And *art museums* being in general so preposterously and insult-
ingly uncongenial to the moods, likes, fancies, tastes of all people
except Roman Emperors, let us for the moment have nothing to

do with them. But rather, drawing our ugliest, most comfortable, chair to the fire-side, putting the foot bench where it fits our feet, pouring ourselves a generous, good long-lasting drink of—what we like, take up this book and, disposing ourselves in the utmost comfort, proceed to—worship? study Art? No. Not a bit of it! Proceed, dear friends, to *like it*.

And now, this very moment—when you with *art laid on your laps* have settled down for the enjoyment of it; when, let us say, those less fortunate than you have journeyed to a public gallery, passed its portals, pushed through its turnstiles, and, with an enthusiasm too soon to be defeated by aching arches, entered upon the inspection of Art—at this very moment, I say, the critic (and that's my role today) if he were or could be, as critic, to any degree a considerate human being, or graced by even the amenity of a Boojum, would "softly and silently vanish away." But critics, sadly, aren't like that. How can they be?

How can they be when, by the very definition of their trade, they have to criticize? Find fault, pick flaws; undo what has been done; tear down, for others—not themselves—to build again. Explain?—the obvious; confuse confusion. And plucking off the petals of the rose, dissect its core—to prove to eyes and nose that beauty isn't beautiful. Critics?

Have any of you listened to the recordings of the poems of E. E. Cummings as recited by the poet himself? And, listening to his clear and resonant enunciation, been both impressed and moved—as I have been—by the beauty of his lines no less than by the simple clarity of his thought? Try it, and be impressed. And yet of Cummings' work a critic writes:

Apart from his constructive destruction he begins the important work of de-anthropomorphization [!] in a brilliantly easeful manner, . . . Anthropocentric man has had, so far, few effective prophets and forerunners and co-operators; . . . Both [and here our critic drags in Picasso, thus relating it all to our subject, painting] know the intelligence and fatuity and pain and necessity of not only disintegrating the ego-sensation, but of putting the bits on any possible hooks, and maybe the derivative hook. The process begins with the stimulus of nausea. . . .

And ends there as far as we, the public, will concern ourselves with such nonsense. Yet this is criticism. And the utter bewilderment of mind which it engenders—and to which an honest few of us most eagerly confess—is identical in kind with that general confusion which criticism—spread by newspapers and periodicals, by lectures, leaflets, books, purveyed by needy hacks no less than by high ranking charlatans, advanced as culture by our "cultured" snobs—has brought to the minds of an honored but too trustful general public. If in America today there is actually in process that wider awakening of interest in the Arts, of which from every hand we have reports, it is largely due to the many forces in our Democracy which, by fostering self-respect in individuals, tend to undermine undelegated authority. It is a wholesome symptom of our coming of age as individuals when we show ourselves impatient of unsought-for counsel. And with all the due honor which we accord to those obligations which, for the good of the many, society imposes upon us, and the respect we feel for the men and women whose social amenities stem from within themselves, there are some things—and not few at that!—which we hold to be, and properly so, our own business. Our thoughts and our opinions; what we like—or don't; what we believe, and how—or whether at all—we worship: These—like his hand to the chieftain Douglas—are our own. We will not tolerate the meddler.

And here am I, privileged by chance to meet you at the threshold of this book: I want your friendship. Yet with me as critic, as one who would tell you which among these pictures you must like, which others you must scorn, with me as an explainer of what, left to yourselves, you'd get at a glance, a disturber of your own thoughts, a dictator of your opinions, an impertinent encroacher upon your own prerogatives, you, if you're wise, will have no traffic. Good, then: I quit!

Only at parting give me one more word. Critic I've tried to be; painter, I am. As a *painter* then, as one who all his life has *worked* at art, one who while critics looked at pictures, worked at *making* them, let me say this: No pictures—*ever*—were addressed to critics: they were made for you. In the simplest and clearest terms that they were masters of, the painters through the ages have recreated life—landscapes and flowers, air and water, human beings and dumb animals, their own thoughts of life and death and all between, their moods, their hopes, despairs, (all these and more are life): they've recreated it. Out of the emotional intensity of their own perceptions they have done this—that others, too, as long as life may last might share their wisdom and their ecstasy.

I'm through. No—one more thought; the last. I want your friendship: let me deserve it then. Discarding both the mantle of criticism and of painting, I come before you in the very clothes which at the moment of writing this I happen to wear: farm overalls. So let me, suiting my actions to my clothes, speak honestly. I didn't choose the pictures in the book.

It is better so; for the choice of them by one vested, presumably, with authority would to some degree have imposed the authority of his judgment upon the reader. Had the selection of the pictures been left to me it would have come to include many that are now in the volume. And with what vindictive fury would it have excluded others! The collection, in short, would have revealed no more than what *I* like. Whereas in its present form it shows what thousands or, for all I know, millions of people like and, in respect to the older pictures, have liked throughout some centuries. Isn't it fortunate that no man or woman may ever have lived who has not for a time at least been loved by someone! In this book there is not one picture that has been less fortunate; and there are many that have been, and forever will be, loved by all.

In the critical commentary which accompanies the pictures, we (for in the commentary I have been assisted by my wise and learned friend, Robert Heller) we have tried—and it has been hard at times!—to not too strongly show our prejudices. What, after all, do any of us *know*—except, perhaps (the wisest of us) what we like. Pretend, if you want to, that you had met us at the door of the picture gallery. And that you had said to us, "Come on in and tell us what you think of the pictures." And that we had gladly accepted. (As, in fact, we would.) Well—these comments are approximately what, trying to be honest and properly respectful of your own opinions, we would have said.

Or pretend that, having met us, you cut us dead, saying indignantly to yourselves, "We don't want anyone to tell *us* what to like!" That would be good too. For after all the only way to cultivate our faculties of appreciation is to exercise them. And we can best do that alone.

Ausable Forks, New York.
1939.

Rockwell Kent

PLATE 1

GIOVANNI BELLINI

1429-1516

Portrait of the Doge Loredano

National Gallery, London

*

VENETIAN SCHOOL

*

GIOVANNI BELLINI was the son of the painter, Jacopo Bellini, the brother of the painter, Gentile Bellini, and the brother-in-law, through his sister's marriage, of the painter Andrea Mantegna. For many years of their lives both brothers collaborated with their father in the execution of his large historical paintings and processional banners. By the example of his family and the influence of Donatello and Mantegna, he came to be himself an important factor in the development of the great Venetian style of painting. Little is known of the details of his life; and although a great volume of the work of his hand has survived the centuries many important paintings known to have been executed have been lost. He was a painter of portraits and of religious and allegorical pictures.

Portrait of the Doge Loredano

By GIOVANNI BELLINI

THE PORTRAIT of the Doge Loredano is the work of the matured Bellini. Here lives for us, to know him and to judge him, the proud tyrant who instituted the Inquisition which for nearly two centuries dominated the life of Venice. Of the portraits of the doges which the Venetian Republic commissioned Giovanni Bellini to paint only this of Loredano survives. The Loredano family was notable in the Republic, having given it many statesmen and several doges. Leonardo Loredano, the subject of this portrait, was born in 1438. He was elected doge in 1501, and died in 1521. The portrait shows him at the age of 67.

Of the school of Venice in the richness of his color, of Padua in the severe precision of his draughtsmanship, Giovanni Bellini's portrait is an unequivocal revelation through the painter's own devout and kindly nature of the essential dignity and kindliness of man.

From the picture in the National Gallery, London
—by permission

IOANNES BELLINVS

PRINCIPAL WORKS BY GIOVANNI BELLINI

Berlin, Museum: "Christ in the Temple."

Boston, Gardner Collection: "Madonna and Child."

Brooklyn, Museum: "Virgin and Child with a Donor," "Portrait of a Young Man."

Cambridge, Fogg Art Museum: "The Madonna and Child" (two versions).

Chicago, Art Institute: "Madonna and Child."

Detroit, Institute of Arts: "Madonna and Child."

Grosse Pointe, Mich., Booth Collection: "Madonna and Child."

Indianapolis, Thompson Collection: "Madonna and Child Enthroned."

London, National Gallery: "Madonna," "Portrait of the Doge Loredano."

Milan, Brera Gallery: "Madonna and Child," "Pietà."

New York, Frick Collection: "St. Francis."

New York, Metropolitan Museum of Art: "The Madonna and Child" (two versions).

New York, Private Collections and Sales Galleries: Many examples.

Ottawa, National Gallery of Canada: "Christ Blessing."

Paris, Louvre: "The Holy Family."

Philadelphia, Private Collections: Several examples.

San Marino, Huntington Collection: "Madonna and Child."

Venice, Academy: "Madonna," "Madonna with Choir of Angels."

Venice, Ducal Palace: "Pietà."

Venice, Santa Maria del Orto: "Madonna."

Washington, United States National Gallery of Art: "The Flight to Egypt," "Bust of a Young Man."

Worcester, Art Museum: "Madonna and Child."

PLATE 2

BOTTICELLI

1444-1510

The Birth of Venus

Uffizi Gallery, Florence

*

FLORENTINE SCHOOL

*

SANDRO BOTTICELLI was born in Florence in 1444. At the age of fourteen he was apprenticed to Fra Filippo Lippi. He remained at this studio for eight or nine years, though it is possible that he also frequented the workshop of Verrocchio.

Early in his career he profited by the patronage of Lorenzo the Magnificent. About this time he painted the famous "Primavera" for Lorenzo's villa. In 1481 Botticelli was summoned to Rome to take part in the decoration of the Sistine Chapel at the Vatican. Thereafter he remained in Florence. Late in life he prepared an elaborate series of drawings illustrating Dante. These constitute the most extensive collection of original drawings from the hand of a Renaissance master.

It has often been suggested that the painters of the Renaissance had some contact with the art of the Orient, yet there is no proof that examples of Eastern art were brought to Italy so early. While it is true that Botticelli's use of linear rhythms is strikingly similar to a practice of most Chinese painting, there is no good reason to believe that he ever saw any of it. It is safe to imagine, though, that if he had, he would have loved it.

The Birth of Venus

By BOTTICELLI

SHE WAS born in the foam of the sea and the Zephyrs carried her along the top of the waves to the Island of Cyprus where the Seasons were waiting to receive and attire her.

Venus, goddess of flowers, of the fruitfulness of nature, goddess of love: she of the Botticelli painting was in fact, or is in legend, the lovely Simonetta, the betrothed of Giuliano de Medici. It is told that, proud of her great beauty, she said to the painter: "I will be your lady Venus; you shall paint me rising from the waves." And it is further told that, realizing as she posed that she was but a model in the painter's eyes, she wept out of injured pride and sent him from the room.

Scraps of legend and invented hokum have preserved the reputation of many paintings that deserve to be forgotten. Botticelli's "Venus" needs no such embellishment. It is "its own excuse for being."

From the picture in the Uffizi Gallery, Florence

PRINCIPAL WORKS BY BOTTICELLI

Berlin, MUSEUM: "Madonna and Child with St. John the Evangelist and St. John the Baptist."

Boston, GARDNER COLLECTION: "Lucretia," "Madonna dei Chigi," "Holy Family."

Cambridge, FOGG ART MUSEUM: "Ecce Homo," "Crucifixion."

Chicago, EPSTEIN COLLECTION: "Madonna and Child with Angels."

Cincinnati, EDWARDS COLLECTION: "Madonna and Child with St. John the Baptist and an Angel."

Detroit, INSTITUTE OF ARTS: "Ecce Homo."

Florence, UFFIZI GALLERY: "The Birth of Venus," "The Calumny of Apelles," "Madonna of the Melagrana," "Fortitude," "Magnificat."

London, NATIONAL GALLERY: "Portrait of a Young Man," "Mars and Venus," "The Nativity," "Adoration of the Magi."

New York, METROPOLITAN MUSEUM OF ART: "St. Zenobius."

New York, PRIVATE COLLECTIONS AND SALES GALLERIES: Several examples.

Ottawa, NATIONAL GALLERY OF CANADA: "Christ Child with Infant St. John."

Paris, THE LOUVRE: "Giovanni Tornabuoni with Venus and Graces."

Philadelphia, JOHNSON COLLECTION: "Portrait of Lorenzo Lorenzano."

Pittsburgh, KAUFMANN COLLECTION: "Madonna and Child."

Washington, THE UNITED STATES NATIONAL GALLERY OF ART: "Adoration of the Magi," "Portrait of a Youth in a Red Cap," "Portrait of a Youth."

PLATE 3

LEONARDO DA VINCI

1452-1519

Mona Lisa

Louvre, Paris

*

FLORENTINE SCHOOL

*

IT IS PROBABLY safe to say that the critics and art historians who developed the legend of Leonardo's unsurpassed greatness as a painter have had the color rise to their cheeks on rereading some of their own straining superlatives. No painter has suffered so severely at the hands of loving critics. The infallibility of his greatness has so deeply permeated our thinking and our judgment that an occasional call for revaluation is regarded either as treason or as part of the stock-in-trade of an habitual iconoclast.

It is true that Leonardo's life was a really great life; that the facets of his genius were innumerable; that his mind was fantastically universal; that he anticipated the modern age. We have the records—his notebooks—to prove all of [*Continued on plate 4*]

Mona Lisa

By LEONARDO DA VINCI

THIS PAINTING, perhaps the world's most famous portrait, has generated more nonsense than any other art-work in history. Thousands upon thousands of lines have been written about it; ecstasies have reached heavenly levels; men have seen in the subject's eyes all of the world that has been and all of the world that is to be. This may be delightful fantasy, enjoyable daydreaming, even good writing—but as criticism it is dense and a sickening pretense.

"Mona Lisa" is an unfinished portrait executed in a manner that was common to many painters of the Italian Renaissance. The picture, in terms of painting itself, is confused in its treatment; it gives the impression of a work whose elaboration was too far extended. The subject is not without psychological interest. The treatment of the mouth, upturned at the ends, makes the subject seem quizzical and curious. Legend has it that Leonardo had musicians present at all times to sustain the peculiar mood of his subject.

From the picture in the Louvre, Paris

PLATE 4

LEONARDO DA VINCI

1452-1519

The Last Supper

Church of Santa Maria delle Grazie, Milan

*

FLORENTINE SCHOOL

*

[*Continued from plate 3*] this. We have contemporary accounts to help us visualize his amazing vitality and activity—as architect, engineer, sculptor, anatomist, and painter.

But what have we today to establish his greatness as a painter? No more than a half-dozen pictures. The largest and most important is in ruins, so much so that nothing at all of the original is retained. Another, his most famous portrait, is an admittedly unfinished work. The remaining pictures are certainly questionable masterpieces. In short, we have no evidence. While it would be pleasant and warming to believe on faith that Leonardo *must have been* a great painter, it is nevertheless a betrayal of honest criticism to make that assumption and then to inflate it inordinately, using doubtful examples to support wishful theorizing.

The Last Supper

By LEONARDO DA VINCI

LOOKING at this picture, we should all be harboring the same feeling—regret. This must have been an excellent painting. Now we can't see a significant vestige of the original. So let's not imagine that it was the greatest of all "Last Suppers." Leonardo did this in oils on an enormous surface, a terrible technical mistake. It was falling to pieces in his own lifetime. A truly great painter of the Renaissance would probably have been a painstaking craftsman.

Leonardo's contemporaries, who themselves had little time to study this picture before it began to disintegrate, were deeply impressed by its design and by the devices Leonardo employed to heighten the dramatic effect. Even today we can appreciate what great technical ingenuity went into the arrangement—the use of converging lines to focus attention on the head of Christ, and the unconventional disposition of his disciples around the table.

Time's ravages and the use of poor materials have robbed us of much that was good in art. If we were to have the miraculous opportunity to recreate some lost works of the Renaissance, surely this "Last Supper" would be our choice. Seeing it in its pristine state would make meaningful, perhaps, what splendid things have been said about Leonardo the painter, things we have had to doubt for lack of proof.

From the picture in the Church of Santa Maria delle Grazie, Milan

PRINCIPAL WORKS BY LEONARDO DA VINCI

London, ROYAL ACADEMY: "The Virgin with St. Anne" (drawing).

Milan, SANTA MARIA DELLE GRAZIE: "The Last Supper."

Paris, LOUVRE: "The Virgin of the Rocks," "Mona Lisa," "The Virgin and Child with St. Anne," "The Adoration of the Magi" (drawing).

PLATE 5

ALBERTINELLI

1474-1515

The Visitation

Uffizi Gallery, Florence

*

FLORENTINE SCHOOL

*

CLOSELY ASSOCIATED with the name of the worldly Albertinelli is that of his intimate friend and collaborator, the saintly Fra Bartolommeo with whom he became acquainted while studying under Cosimo Rosselli. Their partnership was interrupted by Bartolommeo's retirement to monastic seclusion at the death of his spiritual leader, Savonarola. Upon his friend's request, Albertinelli undertook the completion of a fresco in the church of Santa Maria Nuova. The distinction of this fresco brought Albertinelli the commission for that painting which is held to be his chief work, "The Visitation." Meanwhile Bartolommeo may be believed to have been restive in the inaction of his retirement and ready for the acceptance of any rationalization that might permit him with a clear conscience to resume activity as a painter. The realization that his earnings could be contributed to the Dominican Order set him free again to take his brush in hand; and after an interruption of almost a decade the partnership of the two friends was resumed. Albertinelli is reputed to have been as wild and reckless in his life as Bartolommeo was devout, and to have poetically balanced their joint account with God and the world by devoting his share of their joint earnings to the operation of an inn.

The Visitation

By ALBERTINELLI

AND THE angel said unto her, Fear not, Mary, for thou hast found favor with God. And, behold, thou shalt conceive in thy womb, and bring forth a son, and shalt call his name JESUS. Then said Mary unto the angel, How shall this be, seeing I know not a man? And the angel answered and said unto her, The Holy Ghost shall come upon thee. And behold, thy cousin Elizabeth, she hath also conceived a son in her old age; for with God nothing is impossible. And Mary arose and entered into the house of Zacharias, and saluted Elizabeth. And it came to pass, that, when Elizabeth heard the salutation of Mary, the babe leapt in her womb; and Elizabeth was filled with the Holy Ghost: and she spake out with a loud voice, and said, Blessed art thou among women, and blessed is the fruit of thy womb.—LUKE 1.

From the picture in the Uffizi Gallery, Florence

PRINCIPAL WORKS BY ALBERTINELLI

Cambridge, Fitzwilliam Museum: "Virgin with Christ and John the Baptist."

Florence, Academy: "The Annunciation."

Florence, Pitti Palace: "The Marriage of St. Catherine."

Florence, Uffizi Gallery: "The Visitation."

Detroit, Institute of Arts: "The Virgin and St. Joseph Adoring the Christ Child."

Paris, Louvre: "Madonna and Child."

Washington, Smithsonian Institution National Collection of Fine Arts: "Virgin and Child with St. John."

PLATE 6

MICHELANGELO

1475-1564

The Madonna, Child, St. John and Angels

National Gallery, London

*

FLORENTINE SCHOOL

*

IN ENCYCLOPEDIAS and lexicons we find: "Michelangelo Buonarroti: sculptor, painter, architect, and poet." He would not have had it this way. Rather, just "Michelangelo: sculptor." This we must accept if we are to appreciate the meaning of his art.

Michelangelo was like the boy who won't go out to play. A precocious genius, he was always drawing. His father sent him first to the atelier of Ghirlandaio, the painter, and then to Bertoldo, the sculptor. Soon he enjoyed the good fortune that came to all promising young men of the arts in Florence, the patronage of Lorenzo de Medici.

Patronage followed its usual course for those days—commissions in Florence and elsewhere, and finally the summons to come to Rome. Disappointed in the failure of an order to execute a marble tomb for Pope Julius II, he accepted the papal command to decorate the Sistine Chapel. Under conditions unbelievably adverse and difficult, he covered the ceiling of the chapel, alone, with what was surely the most grandiose conception in all of Western painting.

Painting, sculpture, architecture, poetry—these were the facets of his expression, and usually they were active simultaneously. He lived long in a time of plagues and robust living, almost a full century.

The Madonna, Child, St. John and Angels

By MICHELANGELO

DURING the first five years of the sixteenth century, Michelangelo painted a short series of Madonnas of which this London version is typical. He had not fully matured and ripened. Life had not yet thrown him back upon his heels. His preoccupation, later an obsession, with the rendering of the perfection and drama of the human form had not yet seized him. And so this religious painting retains much of the sweet, almost sentimental, quality of his first teacher, Ghirlandaio. There are passages—the draperies covering the legs of the Madonna—which indicate the line of his future development, bold, monumental treatment, painting in terms of sculpture.

From the picture in the National Gallery, London
—by permission

PRINCIPAL WORKS BY MICHELANGELO

London, BRITISH MUSEUM: Drawings.

London, NATIONAL GALLERY: "The Entombment" (not finished), "Madonna and Child, St. John and Angels."

Rome, PAULINE CHAPEL: "The Conversion of St. Paul," "The Crucifixion of St. Peter."

Rome, SISTINE CHAPEL: "The Creation," "The Last Judgment."

There are no well-known works of Michelangelo in the United States, either in public galleries or in private collections. There is some work from his hand. The Detroit Institute of Arts has a study sheet; the Morgan Collection in New York has the sketches for "David Slaying Goliath"; and there is a copy of "The Holy Family" in the Museum of Fine Arts at Boston.

PLATE 7

TITIAN

1482-1576

Bacchus and Ariadne

National Gallery, London

*

VENETIAN SCHOOL

*

TIZIANO VECELLIO, known to the world as Titian, was born in Cadore in the Alpine district of Italy about 1482. He studied under Sebastiano Zuccato, a Venetian mosaicist, and under the brothers Giovanni and Gentile Bellini and under Giorgione. Following his first early recognition as a master, he was to be favored throughout his life by the friendship of the mighty and the great. In 1530 Titian was received with high honor at the Imperial court of Emperor Charles V. He was created Count Palatine of the empire and a knight of the Golden Spur. Great honors these. He was *granted* a pension on the Treasury of Naples from the emperor; but the letters of entreaty and demand with which he bombarded the Treasury are still [*Continued on plate 8*]

Bacchus and Ariadne

By TITIAN

ARIADNE, the daughter of King Minos of Crete, having furnished Theseus with a sword with which to encounter the Minotaur and with a thread by means of which he was to find his way out of the Labyrinth, having, in short, done everything to secure the triumph of the man she loved in the great enterprise which he had undertaken, let herself, eagerly enough, be carried away by him when he sailed to return to Athens. Theseus tired of her; and while she was asleep on the Island of Naxos where they had stopped, abandoned her. Venus came to Ariadne and took pity on her, consoling her with the promise of an immortal lover.

It happened that the island of Naxos was a favorite playground of the god Bacchus. And so it was contrived that as Ariadne sat lamenting her fate, Bacchus came to her. Touched by her grief, he consoled her and made her his wife. He gave her as a marriage present a golden crown encircled with gems; and when at last she died, he tossed her crown up into the heavens. There it became a constellation.

The poet Spenser has written of this happening:

> Look how the crown which Ariadne wore
> Upon her ivory forehead that same day
> That Theseus her unto his bridal bore;
> Then the bold Centaurs made that bloody fray
> With the fierce Lapiths which did them dismay;
> Being now placed in the firmament,
> Through the bright heaven doth her beams display,
> And is unto the stars an ornament,
> Which round about her move in order excellent.

From the picture in the National Gallery, London
—by permission

PLATE 8

TITIAN

1482-1576

Flora

Uffizi Gallery, Florence

*

VENETIAN SCHOOL

*

[*Continued from plate 7*] extant as evidence that for at least many years he was not paid. Titian was endowed with a strong constitution and great energy. Vasari visited him in 1566—Titian was then at least 84—and found him with his brushes in his hand at work. Eight years later he received, with a magnificence for which he was known, King Henry III of France. Titian succumbed to the plague which swept Venice in 1576. To honor the last remains of a great citizen, the law forbidding the victims of the plague to be interred in the churches was set aside. Titian was buried in the Church of the Frari. There in that church by his great "Assumption" and his altar piece, "Madonna dei Casa Pesaro," Titian lives on.

Flora

By TITIAN

"HERE blushing Flora paints th' enameled ground," wrote Pope. She was the goddess of flowers and of blooming vegetation and the beloved of Zephyrus, the wind. Milton, writing of Adam contemplating Eve as she lay asleep, speaks of the love of Zephyrus for Flora:

> *. . . He on his side*
> *Leaning half raised, with looks of cordial love,*
> *Hung over her enamoured, and beheld*
> *Beauty which, whether waking or asleep,*
> *Shot forth peculiar graces; then with voice,*
> *Mild, as when Zephyrus on Flora breathes,*
> *Her hand soft touching, whispered thus: "Awake!*
> *My fairest, my espoused, my latest found,*
> *Heaven's last, best gift, my ever-new delight."*

It is said that Titian's model for Flora was his mistress. And a clerk taking inventory of the property of Peter Paul Rubens listed "Four pictures of Venetian courtesans, after Titian." "Flora" is believed to have been one of them. Vasari records that Titian painted his portraits of ideal womanhood more from imagination than from models. Some of us, looking at "Flora," will believe this.

From the picture in the Uffizi Gallery, Florence

Baltimore, EPSTEIN COLLECTION: "Portrait of a Man."

Boston, GARDNER COLLECTION: "The Rape of Europa."

Chicago, PRIVATE COLLECTIONS: Several examples.

Cincinnati, MUSEUM ASSOCIATION: "Portrait of Philip II of Spain."

Detroit, FORD COLLECTION: "Andrea Navagero."

Detroit, INSTITUTE OF ARTS: "Man with a Flute," "Judith with the Head of Holofernes," "The Appeal" (jointly with others).

Florence, PITTI GALLERY: "The Magdalen," "Head of Christ."

Florence, UFFIZI GALLERY: "Flora," "Venus and Cupid," "Portrait of the Duke of Urbino."

Indianapolis, TARKINGTON COLLECTION: "Portrait of a Man."

Kansas City, NELSON GALLERY: "Portrait of Antoine Perrenot, Cardinal de Granvelle."

Kenosha, ALLEN COLLECTION: "Portrait of the Doge Andrea Gritti."

London, NATIONAL GALLERY: "Bacchus and Ariadne," "Noli Me Tangere," "Holy Family and Shepherd."

Minneapolis, INSTITUTE OF ARTS: "The Temptation of Christ."

New York, FRICK COLLECTION: "Man with a Red Cap," "Portrait of Pietro Aretino."

New York, METROPOLITAN MUSEUM OF ART: "Portrait of the Doge Andrea Gritti," "Portrait of Alfonso d'Este," "Venus and the Lute Player."

New York, PRIVATE COLLECTIONS AND SALES GALLERIES: Several examples.

Ottawa, NATIONAL GALLERY OF CANADA: "Portrait of Daniele Barbaro."

Paris, LOUVRE: "Man with a Glove," "Madonna with St. Agnes."

Philadelphia, WIDENER COLLECTION: "Portrait of Irene di Spilimbergo," "Portrait of Emilia di Spilimbergo," "Venus and Adonis."

Rome, VILLA BORGHESE: "Sacred and Profane Love," "Education of Cupid."

St. Louis, CITY ART MUSEUM: "Christ Shown to the People."

Sarasota, RINGLING MUSEUM: "Portrait of Caterina Cornaro, Queen of Cyprus."

Venice, FRARI: "Assumption," "Madonna dei Casa Pesaro."

Venice, SANTA MARIA DELLA SALUTE: Ceiling pieces, "St. Mark Enthroned," "Descent of the Holy Spirit."

Washington, UNITED STATES NATIONAL GALLERY OF ART: "Toilet of Venus," "Madonna and Child with the Infant St. John Bringing a Lamb to the Child," "Portrait of Andrea Franceschi" (uncertain).

PLATE 9

RAPHAEL

1482-1520

The Ansidei Madonna

National Gallery, London

*

UMBRIAN SCHOOL

*

RAPHAEL'S FATHER was a painter in the employ of the Duke of Urbino. He died when Raphael was only eleven, but it was during this formative period that Raphael received his original impetus and the seed of his future development. It is fruitless to attempt to define Raphael's progressive absorption of external influences. The imprint of Perugino, with whom he studied, was obvious at first, but soon became submerged. Raphael seems to have had the perfect faculty of eclecticism, consciously taking the best of everything and adapting it in a purely personal, unobtrusive way.

Raphael worked first in Urbino and Florence, but his large monumental paintings date from the time of his activity in Rome where, as one of the many painters invited by Pope Julius II to improve the Vatican, he decorated the Stanza della Segnatura with the famous "Disputa," a magnificent, strong conception, and with the "School of Athens," even bolder in design. He was always surrounded by a large retine of pupils who formed a sort of "personal court" about him. During the years in which he was engaged upon these large decorations, Raphael continued to produce innumerable Madonnas, designs for tapestries, portraits, and even architectural designs.

He died on Good Friday in 1520 and was entombed, fittingly, in the Pantheon.

The Ansidei Madonna

By RAPHAEL

THIS altarpiece, painted about 1507, was commissioned by the Ansidei family of Perugia to be placed in the Church of San Fiorenzo. It is in a remarkably fine state of preservation, having lost little of its original freshness of color. The delicacy and minuteness with which Raphael handled detail in this altarpiece recalls the painting of Flanders and is testimony to Raphael's early admiration of the work of Roger van der Weyden and Justus of Ghent.

It is foolish to think of the term "eclectic" only in an unfavorable sense. Mere imitation of another style is, of course, no great achievement. The use of another style to make one's artistic expression personal is more worthy of praise and admiration. Raphael, during his entire development, was always receptive to new influences if they could be adapted and translated to help his painting. This panel shows more than Raphael's admiration for the Flemish painters; it has, too, the unmistakable imprint of Perugino, his teacher. But nowhere is there imitation or mimicry. While Raphael took freely from others, he gave even more largely of his own personal, intimate self.

From the picture in the National Gallery, London
—by permission

PRINCIPAL WORKS BY RAPHAEL

Baltimore, EPSTEIN COLLECTION: "Emilia Pia de Montefeltro."

Boston, GARDNER COLLECTION: "Pietà," "Portrait of Tommaso Inghirami."

Boston, MUSEUM OF FINE ARTS: "Virgin and Child in Glory Worshiped by St. Francis and St. Anthony" (attribution questioned).

Detroit, INSTITUTE OF ARTS: "Two Scenes from the Life of St. Nicholas of Tolentino" (shop of Raphael), "Portrait, presumed to be of Taddeo Taddei."

London, NATIONAL GALLERY: "The Ansidei Madonna," "The Vision of a Knight," "St. Catherine."

New York, METROPOLITAN MUSEUM OF ART: "Virgin and Child Enthroned with Saints," "The Agony in the Garden."

New York, PRIVATE COLLECTIONS: Some examples.

Notre Dame, UNIVERSITY: "Madonna of the Oak."

Paris, LOUVRE: "La Belle Jardinière," "St. George."

Philadelphia, WIDENER COLLECTION: The small Cowper "Madonna and Child."

Princeton, UNIVERSITY: "Holy Family" (by Raphael with assistants).

Rome, VATICAN: Seventy frescoes.

St. Louis, SHOENBERG COLLECTION: "Portrait of a Young Man."

Washington, UNITED STATES NATIONAL GALLEY OF ART: "St. George and the Dragon," the large Cowper "Madonna and Child," and another "Madonna and Child."

PLATE 10

ANDREA DEL SARTO

1486-1531

The Madonna of the Harpies

Uffizi Gallery, Florence

*

FLORENTINE SCHOOL

*

ANDREA D'AGNOLO, or, as he has come to be known, Andrea Del Sarto, was born at Florence and was apprenticed in early youth to a goldsmith. A few years of earnest study were followed by tuition from Piero di Cosimo. His taste for drawing, however, led him to learn industriously from the line works of Michelangelo and Leonardo. His skill in copying the works of the masters and the alleged astonishing precision of his painting gained for him the reputation of "the faultless painter."

In 1518 he went to France at the invitation of Francis I and painted the monarch and many members of the court. Commissioned by the king to return to Florence to acquire works of art for him, the painter launched into a life of dissipation, squandering even the money entrusted to him for purchases on the king's behalf. Stung with remorse and utterly in despair, he died and was buried at Florence in 1531.

The Madonna of the Harpies

By ANDREA DEL SARTO

IT IS significant of no more than the vast number of Madonnas painted by the Italian masters of the Renaissance that an obscure detail of this "Madonna and Child" by Andrea Del Sarto has given the picture its name. Curious, but of no particular interest in the composition, are the little winged female figures of the harpies. They may suggest, if we incline to seek such meanings, the contrast between good and evil.

Choosing, with questionable wisdom, Andrea Del Sarto as a symbol of the artist in his attitude to life and work, Browning has made him say:

> I am grown peaceful as old age tonight.
> I regret little, I would change still less.
> Since there my past life lies, why alter it? . . .
> This must suffice me here. What would one have?
> In heaven, perhaps, new chances, one more chance—
> Four great walls in the New Jerusalem,
> Meted on each side by the angel's reed,
> For Leonard, Rafael, Agnolo, and me
> To cover,—the three first without a wife,
> While I have mine! . . .

From the picture in the Uffizi Gallery, Florence

PRINCIPAL WORKS BY ANDREA DEL SARTO

Boston, MUSEUM OF FINE ARTS: "Madonna, Child, and St. John" (jointly with pupils).

Cleveland, MUSEUM OF ART: "The Sacrifice of Abraham."

Florence, UFFIZI GALLERY: "Madonna of the Harpies," "Self-Portrait."

Florence, PITTI PALACE: "Assumption of the Virgin."

Florence, SAN SALVI: "The Last Supper" (fresco).

London, NATIONAL GALLERY: "The Holy Family," "Self-Portrait."

New York, METROPOLITAN MUSEUM OF ART: "The Holy Family."

New York, PRIVATE COLLECTIONS: Several examples.

Ottawa, NATIONAL GALLERY OF CANADA: "The Magdalen" (attribution not certain).

Paris, LOUVRE: "Charity," "The Holy Family."

Philadelphia, JOHNSON COLLECTION: "Portrait of a Young Man."

Vienna, GALLERY: "The Holy Family."

PLATE 11

CORREGGIO

1497-1534

The Mystic Marriage of St. Catherine

Louvre, Paris

*

SCHOOL OF PARMA

*

CORREGGIO, WHOSE TRUE name was Antonio Allegri, received his title from the city of his birth. He first studied anatomy and then went to the school of Francesco Ferrari Bianchi. It is probable that he studied too with the followers of Andrea Mantegna at Padua.

He married and settled at Parma in 1520. It was here that he executed his two greatest works, "The Ascension of Christ" and "The Assumption of the Virgin," both enormous frescoes designed to cover the cupolas of the Church of San Giovanni and the Cathedral at Parma. From a purely technical point of view, these frescoes are both daring and advanced. Through violent foreshortening, far beyond anything his contemporaries ever ventured, he was able to achieve the wonderful feeling of "uplift" and "floating" in both of these large decorations. There are extant about forty works that can be definitely attributed to Correggio. He received no direct influence from a single personality and left little mark on his pupils. Bernardo Gatti is probably the only one of his followers who deserves mention.

The Mystic Marriage of St. Catherine

By CORREGGIO

IN THIS religious subject, Correggio manifests quite clearly an affinity with the style of Leonardo, chiefly in the painting of the head of the Madonna. There is a softness, almost a lush quality, in the handling of the subject; this "effeminate" treatment is very frequently found in Correggio's works. It is, on the whole, but one example of a growing tendency in Italian painting to soften, at times, sweeten, the religious subject—in short, to humanize it.

Here the representations of the Christ-child, the Madonna, Saint Catherine, and Saint Sebastian are delicate, relaxed, and lyrical. It is a healthy and poetic conception, unmystical and warm. This is no doubt the quality to which literary men were alluding when they spoke of the "correggiosity" of Correggio.

From the picture in the Louvre, Paris

PRINCIPAL WORKS BY CORREGGIO

Boston, GARDNER COLLECTION: "Girl with Thorn."

Brunswick, Maine, BOWDOIN COLLEGE: "Madonna and Child" (drawing).

Cambridge, FOGG ART MUSEUM: "Study for a Head."

Detroit, INSTITUTE OF ARTS: "Mater Amabilis," "Madonna of the Basket," "St. John the Baptist in the Wilderness," "Angels," and many drawings.

Dresden, GALLERY: "Madonna and St. George."

London, NATIONAL GALLERY: "Madonna della Cesta," "Ecce Homo," "The Education of Cupid."

Paris, LOUVRE: "The Mystic Marriage of St. Catherine," "Jupiter and Antiope."

Parma, CAMERA DEL CORREGGIO: Frescoes.

Parma, CATHEDRAL: Frescoes.

Parma, GALLERY: "Virgin and Child with St. Jerome."

Parma, CHURCH OF SAN GIOVANNI EVANGELISTA: Frescoes.

PLATE 12

BORDONE

1500-1570

The Lovers

Brera Gallery, Milan

*

VENETIAN SCHOOL

*

Paris Bordone was born in Treviso. He lived and died in Venice. A pupil of Titian, strongly influenced by Giorgione and others, he lived in the period of the decline of the Venetian Republic and of what had been the most sumptuous school of painting that the world has known. He was of a noble family; yet such was the position of the artist in the community of Venice in that period that his father encouraged him to follow the career of art.

Much of Bordone's work was done for churches. His masterpiece is held to be the large painting known as "The Fisherman Presenting the Ring of St. Mark to the Doge," a work which characterized the Republic in Bordone's time.

After various successes in Italy, Bordone was invited by Francis I to visit France. Here besides executing several commissions for that distinguished royal patron of the arts, he painted portraits of members of the court.

The Lovers

By BORDONE

"THE LOVERS" in the Brera collection at Milan is a well-known example of Bordone's smaller subject pictures.

"The Lovers," writes one critic, "expresses deep and intense feeling." Let us judge of that for ourselves, reminding ourselves, lightly, of the quality of love by these little couplets by George Chappell:

When love is given
Love is heaven.

When love is lent
Love is spent.

When love is sold
Love is cold.

When love is bought
Love is naught.

From the picture in the Brera Gallery, Milan

PRINCIPAL WORKS BY BORDONE

Boston, GARDNER COLLECTION: "Christ in the Temple."

Boston, MUSEUM OF FINE ARTS: "Portrait of Lavinia, Titian's Daughter."

London, NATIONAL GALLERY: "Portrait of a Genoese Lady."

Milan, BRERA GALLERY: "The Lovers."

New York, HISTORICAL SOCIETY: "Repose on the Flight into Egypt."

Paris, LOUVRE: "Portrait of a Man."

Philadelphia, JOHNSON COLLECTION: "Christ Taking Leave of His Mother."

Philadelphia, WIDENER COLLECTION: "The Baptism of Our Lord."

Toronto, ART GALLERY: "Portrait of a Man."

Venice, ACADEMY: "Fishermen Presenting the Ring."

PLATE 13

MORONI

1525-1578

Portrait of a Tailor

National Gallery, London

*

SCHOOL OF BRESCIA

*

THE SMALL GROUP called the school of Brescia was a kind of provincial branch of the great Venetian school of painting, its members having either been trained in Venice or influenced by the Venetian masters. Among the Brescian painters was Alessandro Bonviccino Moretto, or the Blackamoor, a devout and sincere painter of religious subjects; the most famous of his pupils is Moroni, one of the distinguished portrait painters of the Renaissance. While other painters were captivated by the magnificence of Venetian pageantry, stirred by the pomp of an era when history was in the making, impressed, or subsidized by princes and nobles and their women, Moroni, touched apparently by no more than the human dignity of his contemporaries of his own class, faithfully painted them. His portraits unpretentiously conceived, well drawn and painted are among the valued documents of history and art.

Portrait of a Tailor

By MORONI

BUT FOR Moroni and a few others, we of today might not so fully appreciate the dignity and the substantial position of that middle class of the Renaissance which through its skill in the arts and crafts contributed to much to the accomplishment of what the nobles, patronizing them, are celebrated for. The tailor of that period of splendid costume is perhaps to be ranked with the craftsman artists of the Renaissance.

The craft guild movement of the middle ages was the prototype, though not the progenitor, of the craft unions of today. It was the expression of the natural interest of the skilled workers of each of the various crafts in establishing such standards of workmanship and compensation as were consistent with the importance and dignity of their crafts. In the northern European countries the rapid development of *crafts* into *industries* led to the formation of associations headed by such syndics as are the subject of Rembrandt's painting of that name (Plate 23) ; and, with the expansion of commerce, to such modern trade associations as, beyond the exploitation of the craftsman, are not concerned with him.

The slowness of Italy's industrial progress permitted the guilds to retain for a long period their true character; and their membership to continue in the enjoyment of their individual prerogatives and pride.

From the picture in the National Gallery, London
—by permission

PRINCIPAL WORKS BY MORONI

Baltimore, WALTERS COLLECTION: "Portrait of a Lady."

Boston, GARDNER COLLECTION: "Portrait of an Italian Nobleman."

Boston, MUSEUM OF FINE ARTS: "Count Alborghetti and Son, of Bergamo."

Chicago, ART INSTITUTE: "Portrait of Ludovico Madruzzo."

Cleveland, MUSEUM OF ART: "Portrait of a Gentleman and His Wife."

Detroit, INSTITUTE OF ART: "Portrait of a Man with a Ruff."

Dresden, GALLERY: "Portrait of a Man."

Dublin, NATIONAL GALLERY OF IRELAND: "Portraits of a Gentleman and His Two Children."

Florence, UFFIZI GALLERY: "Portrait of a Scholar," "Portrait of a Knight."

London, NATIONAL GALLERY: Portraits of "A Tailor," "A Lawyer," "An Italian Lady," "An Italian Noble," "An Ecclesiastic."

Munich, GALLERY: "Portrait of a Lady."

New York, METROPOLITAN MUSEUM OF ART: "Portrait of Bartolommeo Bongho," "Portrait of a Warrior," "Portrait of Lucrezia Cataneo."

New York, PRIVATE COLLECTIONS: Several examples.

Ottawa, NATIONAL GALLERY OF CANADA: "Portrait of a Man in Black."

Philadelphia, PRIVATE COLLECTIONS: Several examples.

Princeton, UNIVERSITY MUSEUM: "Portrait of a Donor."

Worcester, ART MUSEUM: "The Bergamask Captain," "Portrait of a Musician."

PLATE 14

JAN VAN EYCK

c. 1386 - 1441

The Virgin and Child and Donor

Louvre, Paris

*

FLEMISH SCHOOL

*

IT IS BELIEVED that Jan Van Eyck was born at Maaseyck about 1386 and that he was some fifteen years younger than his less celebrated brother, Hubert. No details of his art studies are known, but his reputation must have been firmly established by 1425 when he entered the service of Philip of Burgundy as court painter. From records of the duke's expenditures it appears that the painter was frequently employed on private missions, but their exact nature can only be guessed. Important among the many works upon which the brothers Hubert and Jan worked together is the famous "Adoration of the Lamb," which adorns Ghent Cathedral.

Not only were the Van Eycks, Hubert and Jan, known by those values upon which true distinction in painting rests; they were important innovators through the introduction into their compositions of actual portraits in three-quarter view meticulously faithful to the characteristics of their sitters, and, through their rendering of light and distant detailed landscapes, the precursors of the realism which was to follow. While they were not the first to employ oil pigments, their use having been known since the tenth century, the Van Eycks developed them to such perfection as to establish them in the favor of the Flemish school.

The Virgin and Child and Donor

By JAN VAN EYCK

"THE VIRGIN AND CHILD AND DONOR" is painted on wood two feet square. It sparkles today with a gem-like luster scarcely if at all diminished since the colors of the Van Eyck brothers were the envy of their contemporaries.

And what a monument to his own unquestionable virtue Chancellor Nicolas Rolin reared when he commissioned Jan Van Eyck to paint him so devoutly kneeling to the Virgin and Child! The likeness is convincing, the piety of Nicolas is impressive, and the memory of this worthy patron of the arts is assured forever. Between the columned arches lies what would appear to be a dream city but the magnifying glass has revealed its details for identification with many of the still existent buildings of Bruges.

There have been many distinguished craftsmen in the arts throughout the ages: the Van Eyck brothers are of their company. There have been none whose craftsmanship has served a more devout, believing, and tenderly perceptive soul than Jan Van Eyck's.

From the picture in the Louvre, Paris

PRINCIPAL WORKS BY JAN VAN EYCK

Berlin, GALLERY: "Portrait of a Man Holding a Pink."

Brooklyn, MUSEUM: "Portrait of a Pilgrim."

Bruges, GALLERY: "Portrait of the Artist's Wife," "The Virgin and Child Protected by St. George."

Leningrad, HERMITAGE: "The Annunciation."

London, NATIONAL GALLERY: "John Arnolfini and His Wife," "Portrait of a Man," "Timotheus."

New York, METROPOLITAN MUSEUM OF ART: "Portrait of a Donor," "Crucifixion," "Last Judgment" (two wings of a triptych).

Paris, LOUVRE: "The Virgin and Child and Donor."

Philadelphia, JOHNSON COLLECTION: "Portrait of a Man," "St. Francis Receiving the Stigmata."

Washington, UNITED STATES NATIONAL GALLERY OF ART: "The Annunciation."

PLATE 15

MEMLING

c. 1433 - 1494

Portrait of Niccolò Spinelli

Musée Royal, Antwerp

*

FLEMISH SCHOOL

*

OF MEMLING'S EARLY youth very little is known, even the exact date of his birth being uncertain. His life, so far as we know it, was tranquil and uneventful and altogether unattended by that tragic poverty and want which has been the lot of numberless men of genius. His great industry, coupled with the regularity of his life, brought him—quite apart from his wife's dowry—considerable wealth and prosperity. It is therefore a little puzzling to discover that not long after his death Memling's name and work fell into such oblivion that only in comparatively recent times was his identity with his paintings re-established.

Between 1470 and 1480 Memling married the daughter of a wealthy burgher of Bruges and became thereby a well-to-do citizen. He purchased a large stone house with two smaller adjacent houses. As time went on his wealth increased; we find his name among those of the 247 richest citizens of Bruges who were called upon to contribute to the expenses of the war between the Emperor Maximilian and the King of France. But the turmoil of the fifteenth century in no degree disturbed Memling's serene outlook. His gentle, peaceful, kindly nature came to live, and lives today, in all that he did.

Memling died on August 11, 1494, at the probable age of 67. He was buried in Bruges.

Portrait of Niccolò Spinelli

By MEMLING

IT WAS the nature of Memling to be moved by only what was good. The splendor of the Flemish Bruges, the opulence of its nobles and great merchants, the famed beauty of its women, the richness of its temporal life, the healthful, deep, unquestioning fervor of its people's worship—all these to him were Bruges. Memling believed it all and loved it. And as a realist who lived in Paradise, he painted it.

To Bruges came many of the leading craftsmen of Europe. Among them was a skilled metal cutter, Niccolò Spinelli, or Niccolò il Fiorentino as he was known in his lifetime. And Memling painted him. None of us looking at a reproduction of this great portrait would suspect that the original panel was but twelve inches high.

From the picture in the Musée Royale, Antwerp

Antwerp, Musée Royale: "Portrait of Niccolò Spinelli."

Bruges, Hospital of St. John: "Arrival of St. Ursula at Cologne," "Triptych of Brother John Floreins," "Diptych of Martin Van Nieuwenhove."

Brussels, Museum: "Portraits of William Moreel and His Wife."

Chatsworth, Duke of Devonshire's Collection: "Triptych of Sir John Donne."

Chicago, Art Institute: "Madonna."

Chicago, Epstein Collection: "King David with a Boy."

Cincinnati, Edwards Collection: "St. Stephen and St. Christopher."

Cleveland, Museum of Art: "Madonna and Child."

Munich, Royal Gallery: "Christ the Light of the World."

New York, Metropolitan Museum of Art: "Portrait of Tommaso Portinari," "Portrait of Maria, Wife of Tommaso Portinari," "Portrait of an Old Man," two examples of the "Madonna and Child," "Christ Blessing," "Betrothal of St. Catherine."

New York, Morgan Collection: "Man with a Pink," and two wings of a triptych.

New York, Private Collections and Sales Galleries: Several examples.

Philadelphia, Johnson Collection: "Christ Crowned with Thorns," "Annunciate Virgin."

Washington, United States National Gallery of Art: "The Man with an Arrow," "Madonna and Child with Two Angels."

PLATE 16

MABUSE

c. 1472 - 1534

The Adoration of the Kings

National Gallery, London

*

FLEMISH SCHOOL

*

MABUSE (JEAN GOSSAERT) was born in the Flemish town of Mabeuse from which he took his name. His life was spent in Antwerp where, at the age of 31, he became Master of the Guild of St. Luke. After a residence of some years in Antwerp, Mabuse entered the service of Philip, bastard of Philip the Good of Burgundy. This service was to have an unfortunate effect upon the school of art which had achieved important national distinction through the work of the Van Eycks. In 1508 Mabuse accompanied Philip to Italy where he acquired those influences which were not only to alter the character of his own art but establish Italy as the field of study for the Flemish painters.

Vasari, knowing of Mabuse's earlier work by hearsay, wrote of the progress that the painter had made in "the true method of producing pictures full of nude figures and poesies," though the pictures as we know them hardly justify that well-meant praise.

Mabuse's later work is of greater distinction, though it is felt that his chief claim to recognition rests on his craftsmanship. He was much in favor with the wealthy patrons of his day, being once commissioned by Christian II of Denmark to paint the portraits of his dwarfs. At the death of Philip, Mabuse designed and erected his tomb. It was under the patronage of Philip's successor, about the year 1534, that Mabuse died.

The Adoration of the Kings

By MABUSE

AMONG the more celebrated of the paintings of Mabuse in his own time was a "Descent from the Cross" on the high altar of the monastery of St. Michael of Tongerloo. At the command of Philip of Burgundy, Mabuse executed a replica of it for the church at Middleburgh. Dürer—such was the fame of the picture—traveled there to see it. He had already seen the great altar piece of the Van Eycks, at Ghent, and written of it in his diary: "A most precious and important painting." Of the Mabuse he noted that it was not so good in design as in execution. This may be taken as a not ungenerous estimate of the work of Mabuse in its entirety.

Whether or not "The Adoration of the Kings" be felt to fall under Dürer's criticism of the Middleburgh painting, it unquestionably yields under Italian influence some measure of that national integrity which, like integrity of character in man, is a precious element of art.

From the picture in the National Gallery, London
—by permission

PRINCIPAL WORKS BY MABUSE

Boston, GARDNER COLLECTION: "Portrait of Anne de Veere."

Brooklyn, PRATT COLLECTION: "Portrait of a Man."

Buffalo, GOODYEAR COLLECTION: "Portrait of a Lady."

Cincinnati, MUSEUM ASSOCIATION: "Portrait of Queen Eleanor of France."

Detroit, HAASS COLLECTION: "Portrait of a Man."

Grosse Pointe, Mich., BOOTH COLLECTION: "Madonna and Child."

Hampton Court, PALACE: "The Children of Christian II."

London, NATIONAL GALLERY: "Adoration of the Magi," "A Man Holding a Rosary," "A Man Holding a Glove," "Portrait of Jacqueline of Burgundy."

New York, HISTORICAL SOCIETY: "Virgin and Child and Cherubs."

New York, METROPOLITAN MUSEUM OF ART: "Portrait of a Man," "Madonna and Child."

New York, PRIVATE COLLECTIONS AND SALES GALLERIES: Many examples.

Notre Dame, UNIVERSITY: "Madonna and Child."

Ottawa, NATIONAL GALLERY OF CANADA: "Portrait of a Man Wearing the Collar of the Golden Fleece."

Paris, LOUVRE: "The Blessed Virgin and Child" in a diptych with "Portrait of Jan Carondelet."

Pasadena, ROMADKA COLLECTION: "St. Jerome Penitent."

PLATE 17

RUBENS

1577-1640

Le Chapeau de Paille

National Gallery, London

*

FLEMISH SCHOOL

*

BORN IN SIEGEN, Westphalia, during a temporary exile of his family, living in Germany until his twelfth year, young Peter Paul Rubens came to Antwerp where he was successively apprenticed to three unimportant masters. At the age of 23 he left upon a tour that took him to Florence, Rome, Mantua, then Spain, then Italy again. Not until eight years later did he return, being honored by an appointment as court painter. He established a workshop, assembled about him a large number of pupils and assistants, and entered upon a career scarcely less notable for the varied activities that it included than for its vast and distinguished achievements in painting. After the death of his first wife, Isabella Brant, in 1626, Rubens entered the diplomatic service of the Archduke Albert and subsequently made several trips to England and Spain. His second wife was Helena Fourment who appears in many of his paintings.

Despite the innumerable and constant distractions which his varied duties entailed, and his genial social gifts invited, the volume of work from Rubens' hand and workshop was immense. He is not only one of the great masters of painting but an enduring influence upon the art of the western world.

Rubens died from gout at the age of 63 at his Castle Steen near Brussels.

Le Chapeau de Paille

By RUBENS

MY MOTHER groan'd! My father wept.
Into the dangerous world I leapt:
Helpless, naked, piping loud:
Like a fiend hid in a cloud.

It might have been of little Peter Rubens' birth that Blake wrote this.

Helpless?—perhaps he never was. But naked! Naked beyond good and evil; naked with the pagan exuberance of the good god Bacchus in childhood; piping?—he trumpeted! Wake up, dead world! You who are oppressed with sorrow, bowed in grief or prayer, solemn in worship, worn from thinking, broken by despair: Wake up! The sun has risen! Life, all life, life bathed in sunlight, in the flesh, is good! Wake up, be happy; live and love. Rubens is the incarnation of impulse, of swift, unreflecting, unrestrained response to life, to the beauty of men and women, their countenances, limbs, flesh, movements, to the world they live in, to the light—so warm and beautiful!—that envelopes them. Loving life so, his brush caressed it.

From the picture in the National Gallery, London
—by permission

Antwerp, MUSEUM: "Adoration of the Magi."

Boston, GARDNER COLLECTION: "Portrait of Thomas Howard, Earl of Arundel."

Boston, MUSEUM OF FINE ARTS: "Rubens' Master and His Wife," "Portrait of Isabella Brant," "Peace and Plenty."

Brooklyn, MUSEUM: "The Risen Christ."

Cambridge, FOGG ART MUSEUM: "Portrait of a Lady."

Chicago, ART INSTITUTE: "Portrait of the Marquis Spinola," "Samson and Delilah."

Cincinnati, CHRIST CHURCH: "The Holy Family."

Cleveland, MUSEUM OF ART: "Triumph of the Holy Sacrament over Folly."

Des Moines, LEHNER COLLECTION: "Ecce Homo."

Detroit, INSTITUTE OF ARTS: "Abigail Meeting David with Gifts," "Philip Rubens, the Artist's Brother," "St. Michael Driving Out the Evil Angels."

Detroit, PRIVATE COLLECTIONS: Several examples.

Hartford, WADSWORTH ATHENEUM: "The Return from Egypt."

Kansas City, NELSON GALLERY: "Portrait of Thomas Parr at the Age of 142."

London, NATIONAL GALLERY: "Le Chapeau de Paille," "Rape of the Sabines."

Los Angeles, Calif., KEELER COLLECTION: "The Duke of Mantua."

Merion, Pa., BARNES FOUNDATION: "Holy Family with an Angel Bringing Fruit."

Minneapolis, INSTITUTE OF ARTS: "James I Designating Charles I King of Scotland."

New York, FRICK COLLECTION: "Portrait of Ambrose Spinola."

New York, METROPOLITAN MUSEUM OF ART: "The Holy Family," "Return of the Holy Family from Egypt," "Madonna and Child," "Adoration of the Magi," "Pyramus and Thisbe," "St. Cecilia," and other examples including many portraits.

New York, PRIVATE COLLECTIONS AND SALES GALLERIES: Many examples.

Ottawa, NATIONAL GALLERY OF CANADA: "Head of an Old Woman," "Christ with the Cross."

Paris, LOUVRE: "Portrait of Elizabeth of France."

Philadelphia, PRIVATE COLLECTIONS: Several examples.

St. Louis, CITY ART MUSEUM: "Portrait of Ambrose Spinola."

San Francisco, CALIFORNIA PALACE OF THE LEGION OF HONOR: "Archduke Ferdinand, Cardinal Infant of Spain" (possibly by Van Dyck).

Sarasota, RINGLING MUSEUM: "The Departure of Lot and His Family from Sodom," "Danaë and the Golden Shower," "Pausias and Glycera" (done together with Jan Breughel the Elder).

Toledo, MUSEUM OF ART: "The Holy Family."

Toronto, ART GALLERY: "The Elevation of the Cross."

Washington, SMITHSONIAN INSTITUTION NATIONAL COLLECTION OF FINE ARTS: "The Holy Family with St. Elizabeth."

Washington, UNITED STATES NATIONAL GALLERY OF ART: "Susanne Fourment and Her Daughter" (challenged as a Van Dyck).

PLATE 18

VAN DYCK

1599-1641

Portrait of Cornelius Van der Geest

National Gallery, London

*

DUTCH SCHOOL

*

ANTHONY VAN DYCK was born in Antwerp in 1599. He was of a good family; and because of the exceptional education which was afforded him, learned several languages. His education, his personal charm, and his polished manners contributed to the winning of that worldly success to which his great gifts as a portrait painter of the rich entitled him. He was a favored pupil of Rubens, their friendship [*Continued on plate 19*]

Portrait of Cornelius Van der Geest

By VAN DYCK

CORNELIUS VAN DER GEEST: That Van Dyck painted him we know. The painting lives. That Van Dyck was paid for his work we may assume. It follows that Van der Geest was a man of means. He was, moreover, a Fleming; and he unquestionably posed for the portrait prior to Van Dyck's departure for England at the age of twenty-one.

Besides Van Dyck's great achievements as a painter he brought into prominence the art of portrait engraving. His prolific accomplishments in both fields is to be accounted for not only by the early mastery of his talent, his indefatigable industry, and the fluent ease of his style, but by his employment of a large staff of pupils and associates.

From the picture in the National Gallery, London
—by permission

PLATE 19

VAN DYCK

1599-1641

Portrait of Charles I

Louvre, Paris

*

DUTCH SCHOOL

*

[*Continued from plate 18*] and mutual admiration being unaffected by the professional rivalry which Van Dyck's early recognition and popularity as a master established. In 1620, when Van Dyck was but twenty-one, he went to England at the personal behest of Charles I. After returning once again to Antwerp and once again visiting Italy, he took up residence in London; and as painter-in-ordinary to the king and favorite of the highest court society lived out his life. Worn out by overwork, he died at forty-two.

Portrait of Charles I

By VAN DYCK

CHARLES I, King of Great Britain and Ireland, second son of James I and Anne of Denmark. His character, weak through inheritance and vitiated by the royal circumstances of his upbringing is to be held in large degree responsible for that succession of events which led through revolution to his tragic end. A weak procrastinator, unscrupulously thankless even to his most devoted followers, obstinate beneath a pretence of compliance, devoutly religious, high-minded according to his feeble lights, virtuous in his domestic life, inordinately proud, weak, dignified, unhappy— all this that we may read in written records, we see in Van Dyck's portrait of the king.

Van Dyck, a descendant in spirit and craftsmanship from the great Venetian masters, a friend and contemporary of Rubens, is the last great master of a school that derived its being from the regal splendor of the feudal tradition. That portrait painting for a century to follow was to show Van Dyck's influence without in any real degree approaching the distinction of the master's work is to be attributed above all to the disappearance of that era of royalty's belief in itself which ended with the Stuarts.

Holding the king's horse in the accompanying Van Dyck portrait of Charles is James Hamilton, third Marquess Hamilton, the king's adviser on Scottish affairs. When the Covenanters banded together, Hamilton courted their friendship in order to betray them. He served both in England and Scotland as the leader of Royalist troops during the civil war. Defeated by Lambert and Cromwell at Preston, and captured, he was tried for treason on the ground that his title as Earl of Cambridge was English. He was beheaded in 1649.

From the picture in the Louvre, Paris

Baltimore, EPSTEIN COLLECTION: "Rinaldo and Armida."

Boston, GARDNER COLLECTION: "Lady with a Rose."

Boston, MUSEUM OF FINE ARTS: "The Entombment," "Portrait of Beatrice de Cusance," "Portrait of Helena du Bois," "Portrait of Margaretha de Vos, wife of Frans Snyders."

Brunswick, *Maine*, BOWDOIN COLLEGE: "The Governor of Gibraltar."

Cambridge, FOGG ART MUSEUM: "Portrait of Alexander Triest."

Charleston, *S. C.*, RHETT COLLECTION: "St. John."

Chicago, ART INSTITUTE: "Samson and Delilah."

Cincinnati, EDWARDS COLLECTION: "Portrait of a Gentleman."

Cincinnati, MUSEUM ASSOCIATION: "Portrait of John of Nassau."

Cleveland, MUSEUM OF ART: "Portrait of Charles I."

Dallas, MUSEUM OF FINE ARTS: "Portrait of Diana, Countess of Oxford."

Detroit, INSTITUTE OF ARTS: "Portrait of a Man," "Portrait of the Marchesa Spinola," "Portrait of Jan Wildens and His Wife."

Grosse Pointe, *Mich.*, BOOTH COLLECTION: "Portrait of the Countess of Buckingham."

Kansas City, NELSON GALLERY: "Rider with Horse."

Leningrad, HERMITAGE: "Portrait of Philip, Lord Wharton," "Portrait of Sir Thomas Wharton."

London, NATIONAL GALLERY: "Portrait of Cornelius Van der Geest."

London, NATIONAL PORTRAIT GALLERY: "Portrait of Sir Kenelm Digby."

London, WALLACE COLLECTION: "Philippe Le Roy with His Wife."

New York, FRICK COLLECTION: "Portrait of Frans Snyders," "Portrait of Sir John Suckling," and other portraits.

New York, HISTORICAL SOCIETY: "Portrait of a Lady."

New York, METROPOLITAN MUSEUM OF ART: "Portrait of James Stuart, Duke of Richmond and Lenox," "Portrait of the Marchesa Durazzo," "Portrait of Thomas Howard, Earl of Arundel, and His Grandson," and other portraits.

Notre Dame, UNIVERSITY: "Crucifixion."

Ottawa, NATIONAL GALLERY OF CANADA: "Christ Blessing the Children," "St. Mary Magdalen in Penitence," "The Death of Adonis."

Paris, LOUVRE: "Portrait of Charles I with Horse and Attendants," "Portrait of the Duke of Richmond."

Portland, *Me.*, REIMAN COLLECTION: "Portrait of a Lady."

St. Louis, CITY ART MUSEUM: "Portrait of a Goldsmith."

St. Louis, SHOENBERG COLLECTION: "Portrait of a Gentleman."

San Francisco, CALIFORNIA PALACE OF THE LEGION OF HONOR: "Portrait of Philip Herbert, Earl of Pembroke and Montgomery."

Toledo, MUSEUM OF ART: "St. Martin Sharing His Mantle with a Beggar."

Toronto, WOOD COLLECTION: "Daedalus and Icarus."

Washington, CORCORAN GALLERY: "Portrait of Charles Lord Herbert."

Washington, UNITED STATES NATIONAL GALLERY OF ART: "St. Martin Dividing His Cloak with a Beggar," "Portrait of Philip, Lord Wharton," "Portrait of the Marchesa Balbi," "Portrait of William II of Orange-Nassau as a Boy."

PLATE 20

DÜRER

1471-1528

The Adoration of the Kings

Uffizi Gallery, Florence

*

GERMAN SCHOOL

*

DÜRER, SON OF a goldsmith of Hungarian descent, was born at Nuremberg in 1471. After a short apprenticeship in the goldsmith's trade he began his studies of art. Dürer worked in Basle, possibly in Strassburg, and later in Venice. Returning to Nuremberg he married; and with the growing burdens of a family applied himself industriously to the making of those engravings for which he is renowned. Of the wide European recognition that Dürer received in his lifetime, of that very special recognition by artists of the achievements of a brother in the arts which frequently characterized the Renaissance, there is no sweeter example than the reception tendered Dürer in Antwerp, as he has himself written of it.

"All their service was of silver, and they had other splendid ornaments and very costly meats. And as I was being led to the table the company stood on both sides as if they were leading some great lord. And there were among them men of very high position, who all treated me with respectful bows, and promised to do everything in their power agreeable to me that they knew of. . . . So when we had spent a long and merry time together till late at night, they accompanied us home with lanterns in great honour."

Dürer died suddenly in 1528 in his native city, deeply mourned by all who had come to know him.

The Adoration of the Kings

By DÜRER

BELIEF in the legend of the visit of the Three Kings to the Infant Jesus was substantiated in the minds of the middle ages by the presence in Cologne of their alleged remains and by the plausible or, for all we know, accurate record of the wanderings of those remains from the time of their first uncovering in Persia in the fourth century. Eleven hundred years, it seems, were pedigree enough. Dürer follows tradition in representing the three kings as of three races and three ages, symbolizing that men of every race and age will worship Christ.

Dürer, carrying on the tradition of the factual Flemish school as established by the Van Eycks, was himself a sound and powerful influence upon the art of northern Europe of his time. A student of Italian art and of the works of antiquity, he was on the whole as little touched by southern influence as the Italians were unimpressed by his paintings. As a painter, Dürer is an important master of the important German branch of the great north European school of the fourteenth, fifteenth and sixteenth centuries. As a wood cutter and engraver he is by virtue of consummate craftsmanship and superb imagination perhaps the greatest master of all time.

From the picture in the Uffizi Gallery, Florence

PRINCIPAL WORKS BY DÜRER

Boston, GARDNER COLLECTION: "Portrait of Lazarus Ravensberger."

Boston, MUSEUM OF FINE ARTS: "Portrait of an Unknown Man," and drawings.

Dresden, GALLERY: "Virgin and Child with St. Anthony and St. Sebastian," "Crucifixion."

Florence, PITTI PALACE: "Adam and Eve."

Florence, UFFIZI GALLERY: "Self-portrait as a Young Man."

London, BRITISH MUSEUM: Drawings, Engravings, Water-color Drawings.

Munich, GALLERY: "The Nativity," "Oswald Krell," "Four Apostles."

New York, BACHE COLLECTION: "Portrait of a Lady."

New York, METROPOLITAN MUSEUM OF ART: "Christ as Salvator Mundi," "Madonna and Child with St. Anne," "Virgin and Child," and drawings.

New York, MORGAN COLLECTION: "Adam and Eve."

Prague, GALLERY: "The Feast."

Toledo, MUSEUM OF ART: "Portrait of the Wife of Jobst Plankfelt."

Washington, UNITED STATES NATIONAL GALLERY OF ART: "Portrait of a Man."

PLATE 21

HOLBEIN

1497-1547

The Ambassadors

National Gallery, London

*

GERMAN SCHOOL

*

HANS HOLBEIN is known as "the younger" to distinguish him from his distinguished but less celebrated father. He was employed for a time in his father's workshop, and then left Augsburg for Basle, then the center of the humanist revival in literature and the home of many eminent scholars of the day. One of them, Erasmus, is said to have been an early patron of the young painter. Holbein remained in Basle almost continuously for twelve years. Then, having won recognition as a master in Switzerland and Germany, and provided with a letter of introduction from Erasmus to Sir Thomas More, he went to England. The introduction served him well, and Holbein soon had access to the leading members of the court. He was appointed court painter to Henry VIII. Of one service to that king our histories tell us. Sent by the monarch to paint a portrait of Princess Anne of Cleves, Holbein, Walpole tells us, "drew so favorable a likeness of the princess that Henry was content to wed her; but when he found her so inferior to her portrait the storm, which really should have been directed at his painter, burst on his minister; and Cromwell lost his head because Anne was a 'Flanders mare,' not a Venus, as Holbein represented her."

---※---

The Ambassadors

By HOLBEIN

JEAN DE DINTEVILLE, ambassador of France to England, is now little but a name in dictionaries of art and biography; Georges de Selve, ambassador of France to the great Emperor Charles V, has the added notation that he was bishop of Lavour.

The Holbein portrait of "The Ambassadors" is obviously an uninspired work; its authenticity is questioned. It brings to mind how cautious we must be of accepting by their label of authorship all of the many poorer or quite worthless works that are attributed to the masters. Homer will nod. Under the pressure of necessity he will descend to work unworthy of himself. He will release from his workshop work that is not of his own hand. Or—and Leonardo's "The Last Supper" is but one of many cases in point—the work of restorers may have obliterated the last trace of the master's handiwork. Let us be cautious, and, in regard to "The Ambassadors," admit it to be unworthy of a master painter's hand.

From the picture in the National Gallery, London
—by permission

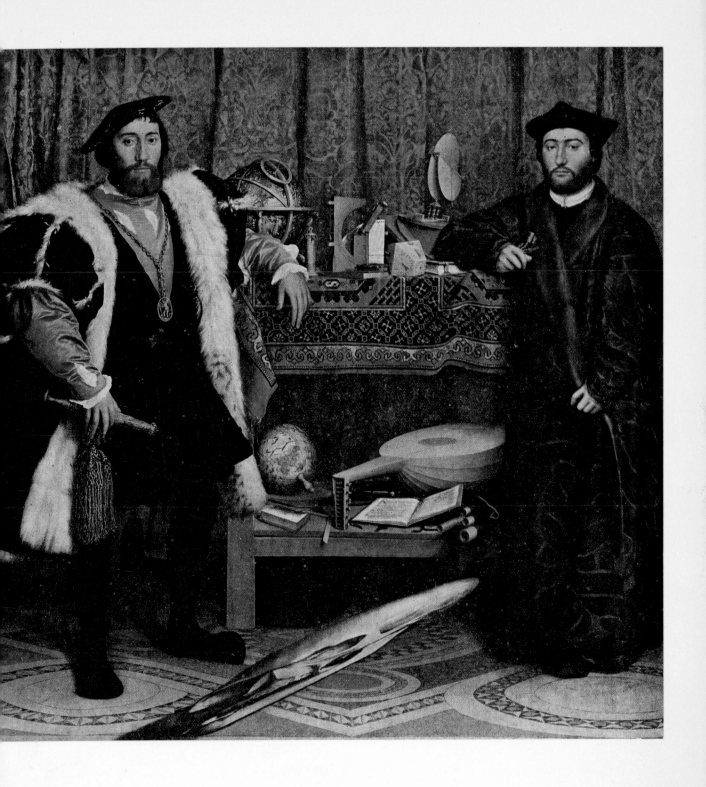

PRINCIPAL WORKS BY HOLBEIN

Baltimore, PRIVATE COLLECTIONS: Several portraits.

Boston, GARDNER COLLECTION: "Portrait of Sir William Butts," "Portrait of Lady Margaret Butts."

Boston, MUSEUM OF FINE ARTS: "Portrait of Sir William Butts."

Cleveland, PRENTISS COLLECTION: "Portrait of Sir Bryan Tuke."

Darmstadt, HESSISCHES LANDESMUSEUM: "Madonna of the Meyer Family."

Detroit: "Portrait of Sir Henry Guildford."

Indianapolis, CLOWES COLLECTION: "Self-Portrait."

London, NATIONAL GALLERY: "The Ambassadors."

London, WINDSOR CASTLE: "Derick Barn," drawings.

New York, FRICK COLLECTION: "Portrait of Sir Thomas More,"

"Portrait of Sir Thomas Cromwell."

New York, METROPOLITAN MUSEUM OF ART: "Portrait of a Man," "Portrait of Lady Rich," "Portrait of Margaret Wyatt," "Portrait of Lady Guildford," "Portrait of Benedikt Von Hertenstein."

New York, PRIVATE COLLECTIONS AND SALES GALLERIES: Many examples.

Philadelphia, JOHNSON COLLECTION: "Portrait of an Unknown Man," "Portrait of Sir John Godsalve."

Toledo, MUSEUM OF ART: "Catherine Howard."

Washington, UNITED STATES NATIONAL GALLERY OF ART: "Portrait of Sir Bryan Tuke," "Portrait of Edward VI as Prince of Wales."

Worcester, ART MUSEUM: "Portrait of a Man."

PLATE 22

FRANS HALS

1580-1666

The Laughing Cavalier

Wallace Collection, London

*

DUTCH SCHOOL

*

MISFORTUNES CONSEQUENT upon the war for Dutch independence led to the flight from Haarlem to Antwerp of the patrician family of which, somewhere about 1580, Frans Hals was born. There is little record of the early life of Frans. He was a pupil for a time of Karel Van Mander, a painter of no distinction. Of Hals subsequent life there has risen such a tradition of riot and drunkenness as is at least inconsistent with the number of his works and the brilliant precision of his style. His first marriage was an unhappy one and after six years he is recorded as being summoned before the magistrates for ill-treating his wife. That her death occurred a few days later has occasioned gossip, but led in its time to no inquest. His second marriage was more fortunate. He lived with Lysbeth Reyniers nearly fifty years and became the father of a large family. That Hals was intemperate there can be no doubt. The charge that he was a sot is ridiculous. To his contemporaries his talents made up for his faults. His portraits radiate kindness and good humor. Hals was, he must have been, a good and understanding man. The poverty in which he died has been the lot of many painters. That it was at no time too great for his endurance is attested by the ripe old age of 86 at which he died.

The Laughing Cavalier

By FRANS HALS

MANY have been the painters who worshiped at the altar of Frans Hals. And with what dismal results! Worship inspired imitation; imitation brought forth artistic atrocities.

Hals used a technique so intimately related to his personality that an attempt to copy his style is like trying to acquire angelic virtues by wearing wings. Virtuosity can be repeated. Hals had more than simple virtuosity. He had character and a unique personality, and expressed both forcefully.

The poor souls who sit and waste their days copying old masters in dimly lit museums, measuring distances and mixing pigments with infinite perfection—let them copy Hals! Square inch by square inch, compare closely the copied color and brush strokes. Miraculously accurate—the original seems reborn. But place the copy beside the true picture and stand back. Then look, and look hard. The gulf is as wide as the difference between life and death.

For Hals had the world's most fluent brush *and* a warm, probing, adventurous spirit. Art hasn't had such a mixture again since his time.

From the picture in the Wallace Collection, London
—by permission

PRINCIPAL WORKS BY FRANS HALS

Baltimore, Epstein Collection: "Head of a Young Man," "Portrait of a Lady."

Berlin, Kaiser Friedrich Museum: "Portrait of a Nurse and Child," "Hille Bobbe."

Boston, Museum of Fine Arts: "Portrait of a Lady," "Head of an Old Lady."

Brooklyn, Museum: "Portrait of a Young Man in a Fur Hat," "Fisher Girl," "Portrait of a Young Lord."

Cambridge, Fogg Art Museum: "Portrait of a Man."

Chicago, Art Institute: "Portrait of Willem Van Heythuysen," "Portrait of Harmen Hals."

Chicago, Private Collections: Several examples.

Cincinnati, Museum Association: "Family Group."

Cincinnati, Taft Collection Institute of Fine Arts: "The Young Man of Haarlem," "Portrait of Michael de Waele," "A Young Woman of Haarlem," "Laughing Boy with a Lute."

Detroit, Institute of Arts: "Portrait of a Lady."

Detroit, Private Collections: Many examples.

Haarlem, Museum: "The Five Regentessen," "The Old Men's Hospital," "The Archers of the Guild of St. Adrian."

Indianapolis, Clowes Gallery: "Self-Portrait."

Kansas City, Mo., Nelson Gallery: "Portrait of a Man."

London, National Gallery: "Portrait of a Woman," "Portrait of a Man."

London, Wallace Collection: "The Laughing Cavalier."

Merion, Pa., Barnes Foundation: "A Dutch Burgher."

Montreal, Private Collections: Several examples.

New York, Frick Collection: "A Burgomaster," "Portrait of a Man."

New York, Metropolitan Museum of Art: "A Youth with a Lute," "The Fingernail Test," "The Merry Company," "The Smoker," "Yonker Ramp and His Sweetheart," "Hille Bobbe," and many portraits.

New York, Private Collections: Several examples.

Paris, Louvre: "La Bohemienne," "Woman Standing."

Philadelphia, Private Collections: Several examples.

St. Charles, Ill., Angell-Norris Collection: "Girl Singing from a Book," "Singing Boy with a Violin."

St. Louis, Private Collections: Several examples.

San Diego, Fine Arts Gallery: "Family Group."

Toledo, Museum of Arts: "Flute Player."

Toronto, Wood Collection: "Portrait of Isaac Abrahamsz. Massa."

Washington, Corcoran Gallery: "Woman with Flagon."

Washington, Dumbarton Oaks Collection: "Portrait of Judith Leyster."

Washington, United States National Gallery of Art: "Portrait of Balthasar Coymans," "Portrait of an Admiral," "Portrait of Nicholas Bergham," "Portrait of an Old Lady," "Portrait of a Young Man."

Yonkers, Boyce Thompson Collection: "Portrait of a Nobleman."

PLATE 23

REMBRANDT

1606-1669

The Syndics

Rijksmuseum, Amsterdam

*

DUTCH SCHOOL

*

REMBRANDT was born at Leyden in 1606, and his family enjoyed enough prosperity to permit him to choose a career. Academic life at the University of Leyden was not congenial. At the age of fourteen he was apprenticed to a Leyden painter named Swanenburg and later to Pieter Lastman, from whom Rembrandt learned the craft without absorbing very much of his master's artistic formulas.

By 1632 his reputation was so well established that he found it expedient to move to Amsterdam. Here commissions awaited him and great demands were made upon his activity. He founded a studio, accepted pupils and assistants, and soon became Amsterdam's most flourishing painter. It was then that he married Saskia Uylenburch, daughter of a wealthy and important family.

Saskia died in 1642. It had been around her that Rembrandt's life revolved, and it was then that he began to drift away from the life of his times. [*Continued on plate 24*]

The Syndics

By REMBRANDT

THE SOLID, serious business men of Rembrandt's Holland, enjoying the fruits of a vast commercial expansion, lived in a world of things that could be touched, and bought and sold. When they had acquired a position in life which commanded the respect of the community, they wished, as all men do, to have a permanent record of their success. If they had no special prominence they thought in terms of their participation in some social or business group. On the whole their mentality was not unlike that of a Chamber of Commerce today in a small American city. Dutch society in the seventeenth century was well integrated; men's common interests brought them together in trade associations and fraternal orders. And frequently, after a new election of officers, they commissioned a group portrait, to be placed on the walls of a clubhouse or in the offices of a trade association.

Thus it was that the five syndics of the Amsterdam drapers' guild came to Rembrandt to be painted. Rembrandt was flourishing then; he was fashionable; to be painted by him was an expression of personal substance and social importance.

These patrons were satisfied with the painting; they were pleased to see themselves pictured with so much dignity and seriousness in their daily job of work. This is no doubt what they wanted in the picture and what they sought when they posed themselves the way they did and assumed an expression of dead seriousness and intense preoccupation with their small world of commerce.

From the picture in the Rijksmuseum, Amsterdam

PLATE 24

REMBRANDT

1606-1669

Man in Armor

Kelvingrove Art Gallery, Glasgow

*

DUTCH SCHOOL

*

[*Continued from plate 23*] The vagaries of his subsequent career—living in common law with the patient, understanding Hendrickje Stoeffels, his financial failure, and abject poverty—have been told and retold with perhaps too much melodrama and more with the adornment of legend than of fact.

As Rembrandt's prosperity and popularity diminished in the later years of his life, the quality of his art improved. The sweep of his brush became broader, his psychological insights became more penetrating, his sense of the dramatic more acute. His later painting was neither understood nor appreciated by his contemporaries; in the strictest sense it should be interpreted as a personal revolt against their canons of taste.

Man in Armor

By REMBRANDT

THAT the painting, "The Man in Armor," is variously known as "Mars" and "Alexander the Great" suggests one of the difficulties which historians of art encounter. Possibly the latter is most accurate; for it is known that an Italian nobleman commissioned Rembrandt to paint an "Alexander," only to complain upon receiving it that it was painted on patched canvas. Rembrandt offered to paint another to replace it; and he doubtless did. At any rate, there are two Rembrandt paintings of this subject in existence: the one here reproduced, and one in the Hermitage in Leningrad.

This is not the type of painting that brought Rembrandt great wealth. It was more the painting that he loved, full of dramatic effect, broad and free in the handling of his brush, sometimes somber and brooding.

From the picture in the Kelvingrove Art Gallery, Glasgow
—by permission

Amsterdam, RIJKSMUSEUM: "The Night Watch," "The Syndics," "The Jewish Bride."

Baltimore, EPSTEIN COLLECTION: "Portrait of an Old Man."

Baltimore, WALTERS COLLECTION: "Portrait of Hendrickje Stoeffels."

Boston, GARDNER COLLECTION: "Self-Portrait," "Landscape with Obelisk," "Christ and His Disciples in the Storm," "A Young Couple."

Brooklyn, MUSEUM: "The Rabbi," "Portrait of Rembrandt's Father."

Cambridge, FOGG ART MUSEUM: "Portrait of an Old Man."

Chestnut Hill, Mass., PAINE COLLECTION: "Portrait of Rembrandt's Sister."

Chicago, ART INSTITUTE: "Christ Washing the Disciples' Feet," "Portrait of a Young Girl," "Portrait of Rembrandt's Father."

Cincinnati, INSTITUTE OF FINE ARTS: "Young Man Rising from His Chair."

Cincinnati, MUSEUM ASSOCIATION: "Portrait of a Young Girl."

Detroit, INSTITUTE OF ARTS: "Head of Christ," "The Salutation," "Portrait of an Old Lady."

Dresden, GALLERY: "Portrait of Saskia."

Glasgow, KELVINGROVE ART GALLERY: "Man in Armor."

The Hague, MAURITSHUIS: "The Anatomy Lesson," "David Playing before Saul."

Indianapolis, CLOWES COLLECTION: "An Old Man in a Tall Fur-Edged Cap."

Kansas City, NELSON GALLERY: "Portrait of a Boy."

Leningrad, HERMITAGE: "Abraham with the Three Angels," "Danaë."

London, BRITISH MUSEUM: "Christ Healing the Sick," "The Three Trees."

London, NATIONAL GALLERY: "Portrait of an Old Woman," "Portrait of a Man," "Self-Portrait," "The Adoration of the Shepherds," "A Woman Bathing."

Montreal, VAN HORNE COLLECTION: "Portrait of a Young Rabbi."

Munich, GALLERY: "The Descent from the Cross."

New York, FRICK COLLECTION: "Self-Portrait," "Polish Rider," "A Young Painter," "Old Woman with a Bible."

New York, HISTORICAL SOCIETY: "Portrait of a Man."

New York, METROPOLITAN MUSEUM OF ART: "Portrait of a Man," "Portrait of Titus," "Self-Portrait," "Old Woman Cutting Her Nails," and many others.

Paris, LOUVRE: "The Disciples at Emmaus," "Woman Bathing."

Rochester, UNIVERSITY: "Portrait of a Young Man."

Sarasota, RINGLING MUSEUM: "Lamentation over Christ," "An Evangelist," "Portrait of a Lady."

Toledo, MUSEUM OF ART: "Self-Portrait."

Washington, CORCORAN ART GALLERY: "Portrait of a Gentleman."

Washington, SMITHSONIAN INSTITUTION NATIONAL COLLECTION OF FINE ARTS: "Portrait of a Man Wearing a Large Hat."

Washington, UNITED STATES NATIONAL GALLERY OF ART: "A Young Man with a Pink," "Joseph Before Potiphar," "Old Lady with a Bible," "Lucretia Stabbing Herself," and several other examples.

PLATE 25

TER BORCH

1617-1681

The Letter

Mauritshuis, The Hague

*

DUTCH SCHOOL

*

BORN AT ZWOLLE in 1617 Gerard Ter Borch was reared in the congenial environment of a cultured family circle. His father was quick in the encouragement of his son's liking to paint and sent him to be a pupil of Pieter Molyn at Haarlem. Years of travel followed for this most favored of the little masters. He visited England, Germany, and Italy in turn. While at Münster in Westphalia he was invited to return to Spain with the Spanish ambassador who introduced him to the life of the court. The portraits that he painted there won him the admiration of an exclusive circle and shortly before his return to his native town in 1652 he was honored with knighthood. While on a visit to England he was introduced into the society of the court and met the great court painter of that time, Van Dyck. Influenced to some degree by the great painters he had met on his travels, he became, nevertheless, the master of a personal style. It is information of a personal and intimate nature that he has given us of the time in which he lived and of that class, the aristocracy, in which he moved. After his death in 1681, his remains were carried to Zwolle where they were interred with great honor amid a gathering of the full citizenship of the town.

The Letter

By TER BORCH

THE DUTCH school of painters of the seventeenth century is noted for the records it has given us of the lives of the people of the upper-middle class of its day. As the Venetian painter, Moroni, supplemented with portraits of the middle class that record of Venetian nobility which other painters of his time so generously supplied, so has Ter Borch completed for posterity the record of the Holland of his day and of his class.

He was, of all Dutch painters of his century, the most cultivated and refined. His horizon was limited by a life spent in the company of the aristocrats and the wealthy. If he knew anything about the existence of his less fortunate contemporaries, the peasants and tradesmen who worked hard and relaxed violently and obscenely, certainly he was careful in his painting to turn his eye the other way. His subjects are all well-mannered, charming people. Their gestures have a narrow scope. Their dignity is always carefully guarded. Never do they "let down their hair."

Ter Borch was the scion of a distinguished family and devoted his art to copying that fraction of the life of his times to which he was born and below which he never stooped.

From the picture in the Mauritshuis, The Hague

PRINCIPAL WORKS BY TER BORCH

Amsterdam, MUSEUM: "Paternal Counsel," "Portrait of Geertjen Matthijssen."

Antwerp, MUSEUM: "The Mandolin Player."

Boston, GARDNER COLLECTION: "The Music Lesson."

Brooklyn, MUSEUM: "Lady Pouring Wine."

Chicago, ART INSTITUTE: "The Music Lesson."

Cincinnati, HANNA COLLECTION: "Portrait of a Cavalier."

Cincinnati, MUSEUM ASSOCIATION: "A Music Party."

Cleveland, PRENTISS COLLECTION: "Portrait of a Lady Standing."

Detroit, INSTITUTE OF ART: "A Man Reading a Letter."

Dresden, GALLERY: "The Officer and the Trumpeter," "Young Lady Playing the Lute," "Young Lady in White Satin."

Haarlem, MUSEUM: "Portraits of Heer and Vrouw Colenbergh."

The Hague, MAURITSHUIS: "The Letter," "Self-Portrait."

London, NATIONAL GALLERY: "The Music Lesson," "The Peace of Münster," "Portrait of a Man."

Montreal, PRIVATE COLLECTIONS: Some examples.

Munich, GALLERY: "The Trumpeter and the Letter."

New York, FRICK COLLECTION: "Portrait of a Lady."

New York, METROPOLITAN MUSEUM OF ART: "Lady Playing the Theorbo," "Young Girl at Her Toilet."

New York, PRIVATE COLLECTIONS AND SALES GALLERIES: Several examples.

Paris, LOUVRE: "The Music Lesson," "Soldier Offering Money to a Young Woman," "The Concert."

Philadelphia, PRIVATE COLLECTIONS: Several examples.

Washington, CORCORAN GALLERY: "Portrait of a Young Man."

Washington, UNITED STATES NATIONAL GALLERY OF ART: "Interior Scene."

PLATE 26

DE HOOCH

1629 - c. 1683

Interior of a Dutch House

National Gallery, London

*

DUTCH SCHOOL

*

FOR MANY YEARS, before scholars really got to work on the facts of his life, it was impossible to arrive at any biographical conclusion about the one Pieter De Hooch who painted the pictures reproduced here. Holland, early in the seventeenth century, had Pieter De Hooch's in most of her larger towns. An unsuspecting historian, using contemporary records as his guide, would have found his subject an amazing personality, coexisting in five places at times, member of almost all the guilds. Sound research at last has gathered together a few important facts about this Pieter De Hooch.

He was born in Rotterdam in 1629 and studied first with the [*Continued on plate 27*]

Interior of a Dutch House

By DE HOOCH

DUTCH homes in the seventeenth century were a tribute to the quiet restraint and dignity that have always characterized the lives and manners of the people of Holland.

Holland then was a rich land, thriving in commerce, abundant in comforts and the things that make everyday living a tolerable, pleasant routine. Another nation, in such favorable circumstances, might have succumbed to the extravagant, superficial pleasures of elegance. The Dutch valued simplicity and comfort. Their homes were uncomplicated, sparsely furnished, full of light playing upon broad, unrelieved surfaces. The pictures of De Hooch reflect this simplicity of living and are a faithful record of the exemplary manners of his contemporaries.

There is, in this painting, a very amusing oversight. Evidently the servant entering at the right, a hurried afterthought, was quickly and carelessly painted. Close examination will show the tiled floor coming through her voluminous skirts.

From the picture in the National Gallery, London
—by permission

PLATE 27

DE HOOCH

1629 - c. 1683

Courtyard of a Dutch House

National Gallery, London

*

DUTCH SCHOOL

*

[*Continued from plate 26*] painter, Berchem, at Haarlem. At the age of 24 he entered the service, as painter and valet (!), of one Justice de la Grange, accompanying his master to Delft, The Hague, and Leyden. From 1654 to 1657 he was a member of the painters' guild at Delft where, together with Vermeer and others, he became identified with a group of artists who painted domestic scenes from Dutch life. After his wife's death, he left Delft in 1667 and moved to Amsterdam. Contemporary records show that he was still living there, in poor circumstances, in 1683.

That is about all we know of the life of Pieter De Hooch.

Courtyard of a Dutch House

By DE HOOCH

OF A CERTAIN class of paintings Ruskin had this to say, "They are good furniture pictures, unworthy of praise, and undeserving of blame." One should not conclude from this remark that Ruskin was a tolerant critic; he certainly was not. What he meant was this. Some paintings, being neither pretentious nor bold, acknowledge their own limitations. They obviously are not inspiring; they tell us nothing about history or mythology; they have no connection with the painter's religion or beliefs. They are only what they seem to be: the products of good craftsmanship, nicely colored, well fitted to be placed on simple walls, to be decorative, and not too prominent.

And so it is with this picture. It is not necessary to be technical about it. Its subject has no mystery; its design has no intricacy. When one of De Hooch's townsmen bought a picture like this, he probably derived as much pleasure looking at it as we do when, going leisurely through an album, we run across a photograph of ourselves and a friend standing in the garden outside our home. It is a faithful scene of familiar people doing familiar things. For legend has it that the woman and child were the painter's wife and daughter.

From the picture in the National Gallery, London
—by permission

PRINCIPAL WORKS BY DE HOOCH

Amsterdam, MUSEUM: "Self-Portrait," "The Buttery Hatch."

Berlin, GALLERY: "A Dutch Interior."

Boston, MUSEUM OF FINE ARTS: "Dutch Interior."

Brooklyn, MUSEUM: "The Flower Garden."

Cincinnati, HANNA COLLECTION: "The Game of Skittles."

Copenhagen, GALLERY: "A Family Party," "An Interior."

Detroit, INSTITUTE OF ARTS: "Mother Nursing Her Child."

Glen Ridge, N. J., BLANK COLLECTION: "Interior with Soldiers in a Tavern."

The Hague, STEENGRACHT: "A Musical Party."

London, NATIONAL GALLERY: "Interior of a Dutch House," "Courtyard of a Dutch House," "Brick-paved Courtyard of a Dutch House," "Dutch Interior."

Minneapolis, INSTITUTE OF ARTS: "Dutch Interior."

Munich, GALLERY: "Dutch Interior."

New York, FRICK COLLECTION: "Girl and Two Officers."

New York, METROPOLITAN MUSEUM OF ART: "The Visit," "Scene in a Courtyard," "The Maid Servant."

New York, PRIVATE COLLECTIONS AND SALES GALLERIES: Several examples.

Paris, LOUVRE: "Dutch Interior Showing Two Women and Child," "Dutch Interior Showing Card Players."

Philadelphia, JOHNSON COLLECTION: "View of Delft after the Explosion of 1654," "Cavalier with a Pipe," "A Group in a Barn," "A Dinner Party on a Terrace," "A Lady Feeding a Child, with a Serving Maid."

Philadelphia, WIDENER COLLECTION: "The Bedroom," "Woman and Child in a Courtyard."

Pittsfield, Mass., MUSEUM OF NATURAL HISTORY AND ART: "The Music Party."

St. Louis, CITY ART MUSEUM: "The Skittles Players."

Toledo, MUSEUM OF ART: "Interior."

Toledo, WILLYS COLLECTION: "A Musical Party."

Washington, UNITED STATES NATIONAL GALLERY OF ART: "Interior," "Courtyard Scene."

Worcester, ART MUSEUM: "The Young Mother."

PLATE 28

METSU

1630-1667

The Music Lesson

National Gallery, London

*

DUTCH SCHOOL

*

GABRIEL METSU was born at Leyden in 1630. He was one of the first to register in the newly formed Guild of St. Luke in his native city, being only twenty at the time. Houbraken, the prolific and frequently unreliable chronicler of the Dutch painters, says that Metsu studied with Gerard Dow in his early years. But after moving to Amsterdam in 1650 he came directly under the influence of Rembrandt. He made an awkward attempt to paint religious pictures, but soon realized that sacred subjects were not his forte. And so he turned to the scenes of Dutch life for which he is famous. Metsu, more than any other painter of his times, cut across class lines in his choice of subjects. They range from the most decorous of family group portraits to the Rabelaisian rowdiness of the peasantry. Metsu married in 1659 and became a permanent citizen of Amsterdam. It was there that he died at the early age of thirty-seven.

The Music Lesson

By METSU

METSU painted high life and low life without moralizing about either. Here is one of the most genteel of his canvases, as fragile and delicate in tone as it is in anecdote.

It is not very often that we find three paintings within the compass of a single frame. Hanging on the wall in the background is a Ruysdael landscape. Beside it is a much larger canvas, "The Twelfth Night Feast" by Metsu himself; two versions of this picture are now in Philadelphia. The Dutch painters frequently used pictures as backgrounds, not in the nature of a joke or trick, but as elements of design and composition.

From the picture in the National Gallery, London
—by permission

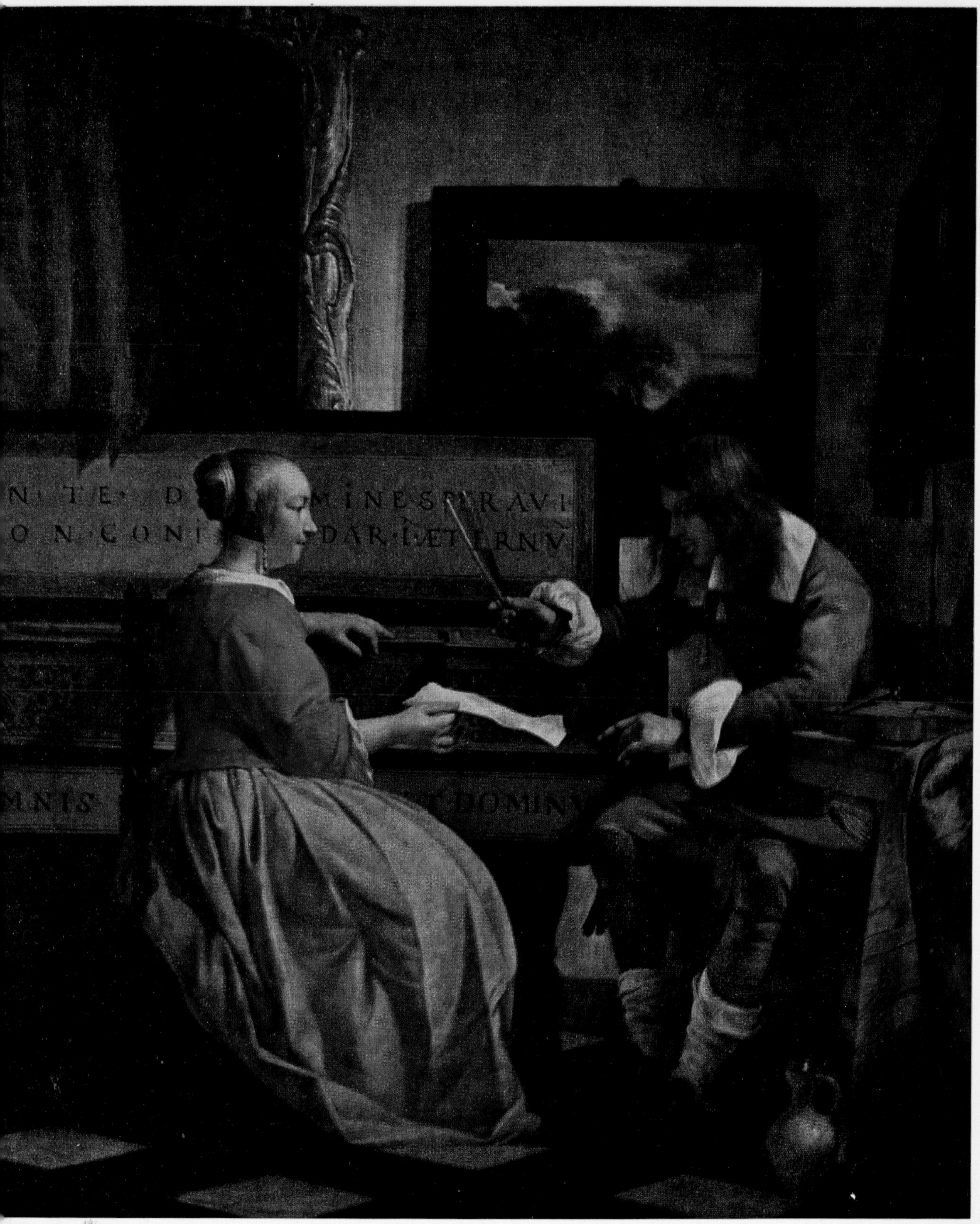

PRINCIPAL WORKS BY METSU

Baltimore, WALTERS COLLECTION: "The Message."

Boston, MUSEUM OF FINE ARTS: "The Usurer."

Brooklyn, MUSEUM: "A Dutch Interior."

Cincinnati, HANNA COLLECTION: "Lady Seated With A Dog."

The Hague, GALLERY: "The Huntsman," "Justice Protecting the Widow and Orphan," "The Amateur Musicians."

London, NATIONAL GALLERY: "The Music Lesson," "The Duet," "The Drowsy Landlady."

New York, FRICK COLLECTION: "Lady in Blue."

New York, METROPOLITAN MUSEUM OF ART: "The Music Lesson," "The Visit to the Baby," "The Artist and His Wife," "The Music Party."

New York, PRIVATE COLLECTIONS AND SALES GALLERIES: Several examples.

Paris, LOUVRE: "An Officer Entertaining a Young Lady," "The Chemist at the Window."

Philadelphia, JOHNSON COLLECTION: "The Hay Barn," "A Young Lady Sewing," "Twelfth Night."

Philadelphia, WANAMAKER COLLECTION: "Twelfth Night."

Washington, UNITED STATES NATIONAL GALLERY OF ART: "The Intruder."

PLATE 29

VERMEER

1632-1675

View of Delft

Mauritshuis, The Hague

*

DUTCH SCHOOL

*

VERMEER'S LIFE fared as poorly as his reputation. He was born in Delft, married in Delft, raised a large family in Delft, painted in Delft. But the people of Delft had little use for his pictures; the pictures didn't sell. And so Vermeer died in Delft, a poor, well-intentioned artist who had the hard luck of being a failure.

One hundred years ago the name Vermeer meant nothing in the history of painting. His works were not known and were attributed to inferior [Continued on plate 30]

View of Delft

By VERMEER

THIS landscape is believed to be an early work, for the brush-work is comparatively broad and free. It is probable that the picture was painted direct from observation, contrary to the custom of that period. Most Dutch landscape painters first made drawings and sketches of their scene, and painted from them in their studios.

The cities of Holland have changed very little during the past few hundred years. If you study this reproduction well and then go to visit Delft, no doubt you will feel at home. Perhaps you will even recognize Rotterdam Gate and the Niewkerk.

From the picture in the Mauritshuis, The Hague

PLATE 30

VERMEER

1632-1675

Lady at a Spinet

National Gallery, London

*

DUTCH SCHOOL

*

[*Continued from plate 29*] painters with more impressive names. After hundreds of years of neglect, a new personality was admitted to art's arbitrary Hall of Fame.

So it was and is with Vermeer. His name today is among the foremost in the history of Dutch painting. His works, small in number, are as precious as jewels. That he could not find a market for his work in Delft is a fact we regret and can do nothing about. But it is a good and encouraging thing to know that effective research and sound appreciation can regenerate a deserving artistic ghost.

Lady at a Spinet

By VERMEER

THIS is a late work, "tight" in handling, more meticulous in detail. The room is bathed in atmosphere; color is subdued and harmonious. It is genre painting at the level of highest perfection.

Vermeer is *par excellence* a painter's painter. As a craftsman he has never been surpassed. And no other painter has so beautifully and correctly organized color in terms of light. Vermeer, unlike Ter Borch and De Hooch, was not interested in the superficial, flashy sheen of textures. He studied the effects of light, captured the play of it upon colored surfaces existing in space and atmosphere, and by painting deliberately and scientifically in the mode of the total visual effect, achieved tonal harmony and richness and delicacy that have never been equaled. His paintings are small and unpretentious; their limitations are acknowledged. They possess the quiet beauty, dignity, and lucidity of well-fashioned gems, and are among the most precious things we have in oils.

From the picture in the National Gallery, London
—by permission

PRINCIPAL WORKS BY VERMEER

Berchtesgaden, HITLER COLLECTION: "The Artist in His Studio."

Boston, GARDNER COLLECTION: "The Concert."

Cincinnati, EDWARDS COLLECTION: "Portrait of a Woman."

Dresden, STATE PICTURE GALLERY: "The Young Courtesan."

The Hague, MAURITSHUIS: "View of Delft," "Head of a Young Girl."

The Hague, RIJKSMUSEUM: "The Love Letter," "A Girl Reading a Letter," "A Maidservant Pouring Milk."

London, BEIT COLLECTION: "A Love Letter."

London, NATIONAL GALLERY: "A Family Group," "A Lady at a Spinet."

London, WALLACE COLLECTION: "A Boy with Pomegranates."

London, WINDSOR CASTLE: "Lady and Gentleman at a Spinet."

New York, FRICK COLLECTION: "The Soldiers and the Laughing Girl," "A Lady and a Maidservant," "The Music Lesson."

New York, METROPOLITAN MUSEUM OF ART: "Allegory of the New Testament," "A Lady with a Lute," "A Young Lady Opening a Casement," "A Young Woman with a Water Jug," "A Girl Asleep."

New York, PRIVATE COLLECTIONS AND SALES GALLERIES: Several examples.

Philadelphia, PRIVATE COLLECTIONS: Several examples.

Washington, UNITED STATES NATIONAL GALLERY OF ART: "The Smiling Girl," "The Lace Maker," "The Girl in the Red Hat."

PLATE 31

MAES

1632-1693

The Idle Servant

National Gallery, London

*

DUTCH SCHOOL

*

Nicholas Maes was born in the Dutch city of Dordrecht. At the age of eighteen he went to Amsterdam where he became one of the many pupils and assistants in the atelier of Rembrandt. It was here that he acquired the warmth of color which characterizes his early genre pictures. The years between 1655 and 1665 were the most productive of his life. The paintings dating from this period are small, simple scenes portraying people engaged in domestic pursuits. When he settled in Antwerp about 1670, his style was radically altered. Possibly under the influence of Van Dyck, Maes abandoned scenes of home life and devoted himself exclusively to portraiture. So completely altered was the matter and the manner of his work that for many years it was believed that two painters named Maes were living at the same time, one in Dordrecht, the other in Brussels. Commissions came readily from the prosperous citizens of Antwerp who were more interested in life-like portraits than in qualities of color and design. At the age of sixty-one Maes died in the city of Antwerp.

The Idle Servant

By MAES

DRUDGERY is a burden and housework day in and day out a bore. The hours are long. Rooms are cleaned, only to be cleaned again. Dishes are washed, only to be dirtied at the next meal. And so, in all ages, servants have sometimes slept at their work.

The ladies of Holland had their domestic problems too. You had to be snapping at servants constantly, watching them every minute, to get things done. It was easy for a Dutch housewife of the seventeenth century to see the humor of this unpretentious little drama. She would not be bitter about things like this. As a matter of fact, she seems quietly amused. Chatting in her parlor with her neighbor's wife, she might point to this painting, shrug her shoulders and say, "It is so hard these days, my dear friend, to keep a house running smoothly. I don't think our husbands appreciate what we must put up with to make them comfortable. But what is to be done to these lazy girls?"

Pictures like this were not made to be placed in museums or described at great length in encyclopedias. Men painted them to sell them. And if they amused people, people bought them and kept them in their homes. And saw them and were amused because— look! that very thing happened to me yesterday!

From the picture in the National Gallery, London
—by permission

PRINCIPAL WORKS BY MAES

Amsterdam, RIJKSMUSEUM: "Girl at a Window," "Old Woman Spinning."

Baltimore, BURNS COLLECTION: "Portrait of Henrietta Maria."

Boston, MUSEUM OF FINE ARTS: "The Jealous Husband," "Portrait of a Lady."

Brussels, ROYAL MUSEUM: "Old Woman Reading."

Chicago, ART INSTITUTE: "Portrait of an Old Lady."

Cincinnati, HANNA COLLECTION: "Titus, Rembrandt's Son, as a Child."

Hartford, WADSWORTH ATHENEUM: "Portrait of Prince Charles, Earl of Plymouth."

London, NATIONAL GALLERY: "The Dutch Housewife," "Portrait of a Girl," "The Cradle," "The Idle Servant."

New York, METROPOLITAN MUSEUM OF ART: "A Woman Making Lace," "Young Girl Peeling an Apple," "Portrait of a Woman," "Portrait of a Young Man."

New York, PRIVATE COLLECTIONS AND SALES GALLERIES: Several examples.

Philadelphia, JOHNSON COLLECTION: "The Lovers," "Kitchen, with a Maid Peeling Apples, and a Pig's Carcass," "Old Woman."

Toledo, MUSEUM OF ART: "Portrait of a Gentleman," "A Lady by a Fountain."

Washington, SMITHSONIAN INSTITUTION NATIONAL COLLECTION OF FINE ARTS: "A Burgomaster."

Washington, UNITED STATES NATIONAL GALLERY OF ART: "Old Woman Dozing over Her Bible."

Worcester, ART MUSEUM: "Interior with an Old Lady."

PLATE 32

HOBBEMA

1638-1709

The Avenue

National Gallery, London

*

DUTCH SCHOOL

*

HOBBEMA WAS PROBABLY born in Amsterdam. In 1668 he married Geltie Vinck, a servant maid four years his senior; by her he had a son and two daughters. Through her influence he obtained a post in the wine office of the Excise. The little stipend derived from his employment scarcely relieved the poverty which beset him all his life. His period of activity as an artist was brief, eleven years. He was a painter of the pleasant countryside of Holland, of red roofed houses, canals, streams, watermills. Always a landscape painter, it was recorded that the human figures incidental to his compositions were painted by his friends, Ruysdael and Van de Velde. Hobbema died in poverty at the age of 70.

The Avenue

By HOBBEMA

HOBBEMA, despite the short period of his activity as a painter, is next to Ruysdael the most distinguished of the Dutch landscape painters. While neither were effective in establishing a school of landscape painting in Holland, their influence upon Constable, the founder of the English landscape school, is definite.

Hobbema's interest in painting the countryside of Holland as every day it met his eyes was kindred to the interest and avowed purpose of Constable in portraying his own England. What to Hobbema and Constable was significant in that it was commonplace, became to their followers (see David Cox, Plates 69 and 70) the "picturesque," and, as such, a ready-made-to-order subject matter for the art of the degenerated heirs of a worthy tradition.

Whether or not the works of Hobbema were studied by the impressionists of the nineteenth century, he reveals a spiritual kinship to them in the outdoor light and atmosphere for which his paintings are noteworthy.

From the picture in the National Gallery, London
—by permission

Amsterdam, MUSEUM: "A Water Mill."

Antwerp, GALLERY: "A Water Mill."

Brooklyn, MUSEUM: "Ruins of Kostverloren Castle on the Amstel."

Chicago, ART INSTITUTE: "The Water Mill with a Great Red Roof."

Cincinnati, TAFT COLLECTION INSTITUTE OF FINE ARTS: "Landscape with Cattle and Figures."

Cleveland, PRENTISS COLLECTION: "A Wooded Lake with a Large Pool."

Detroit, INSTITUTE OF ARTS: "A River Scene."

Glasgow, GALLERY: "A Group of Trees," "Wooded Landscape," "Landscape in a Storm."

Indianapolis, JOHN HERRON ART INSTITUTE: "Landscape with Cottages."

Kansas City, NELSON GALLERY: "Road in the Woods."

London, NATIONAL GALLERY: "Woody Landscape," "Village with Water Mills," "Ruins of Brederode Castle," "Forest Scene," "Castle in a Rocky Landscape," "The Avenue, Middelharnis."

Madison, N. J., TILGHMAN COLLECTION: "Old Mill."

New York, FRICK COLLECTION: "View of a Woody Country," "Landscape with Buildings and Figures."

New York, METROPOLITAN MUSEUM OF ART: "Entrance to a Village."

New York, PRIVATE COLLECTIONS AND SALES GALLERIES: Many examples.

Paris, LOUVRE: "Landscape."

Philadelphia, MUSEUM OF ART: "Wooded Road."

Philadelphia, PRIVATE COLLECTIONS: Several examples.

Pittsburgh, PRIVATE COLLECTIONS: Several examples.

Saugatuck, Conn., ENO COLLECTION: "The Water Mill."

Washington, CORCORAN GALLERY: "Landscape with Figures and Ruins."

Washington, UNITED STATES NATIONAL GALLERY OF ART: "The Farm in the Sun," "The Holford Landscape," "The Farmyard."

PLATE 33

VELASQUEZ

1599-1660

Venus and Cupid

National Gallery, London

*

SPANISH SCHOOL

*

AT THIRTEEN THE young Velasquez was a pupil of the Spanish painter and fa-
natical tyrant, Francisco Herrera the elder. Surviving this, he went a year later to study
under the polished and scholarly Francisco Pacheco. Here, privileged no doubt to
mingle with the nobles and intellectuals who frequented Pacheco's house, he remained
for five years, winning from his master the first recognition of an original and personal
talent. Probably less through instruction than by natural tendency Velasquez was a
realist, his conviction that art must follow nature deepening as his life advanced. The
apparent similarity of Velasquez's manner of painting to that of [Continued on plate 34]

Venus and Cupid

By VELASQUEZ

IT WAS no doubt a problem to one whose rank was that of Grand Marshal of the Palace in a Court noted for its sober dignity to paint the goddess Venus, full length, full faced, and unadorned, and yet in painting her preserve to some extent her modesty, and spare a prudish Court its blushes. That problem Velasquez, with a mirror, solved. And the picture, owned at one time by the Merritt family of Rokeby, is now known as the "Rokeby Venus."

Although the art of painting is ostensibly limited to the *appearance* of life, the painter-seer (and all great masters of the art are that) views surfaces as but the covering of underlying structural truth or principle. Under the forest-clad slopes that meet our eyes the seer perceives the naked contours of the earth; behind the mask of the human countenance he discerns essential character; and beneath the voluminous brocades and satins, the hoops and panniers of whalebone and steel, the bales of petticoats that made, to courtiers' eyes, a Spanish lady there lived, though who would guess it, the primordial woman, call her Eve or Venus.

From the picture in the National Gallery, London
—by permission

33

PLATE 34

VELASQUEZ

1599-1660

Portrait of Philip IV

National Gallery, London

*

SPANISH SCHOOL

*

[*Continued from plate 33*] his slightly older contemporary, Ribera, has led some authorities to term imitation what was in fact a spiritual likeness between the two. Velasquez, a great master of realism, came to have a profound influence on European art of the succeeding centuries.

In 1618 Velasquez married his master's daughter, Juana; and four years later, being already the father of two daughters, the family accompanied by Pacheco himself journeyed to Madrid. Here but for two journeys to Italy he was to spend his life. Under the royal patronage and favor he rose to that high rank of Grand Marshal of the Palace which, through the obligations and restraints that it imposed, was to curtail the painter's output at the very height of his powers. It was in the fatiguing performance of his distinguished official duties that he died.

Portrait of Philip IV

By VELASQUEZ

OF THE "shattered visage" of one Ozymandias who had held himself to be the "king of kings" Shelley wrote

> . . . *whose frown*
> *And wrinkled lip and sneer of cold command*
> *Tell that its sculptor well those passions read*
> *Which yet survive, stamped on those lifeless things,*
> *The hand that mocked them and the heart that fed* . . .
> *Nothing beside remains. Round the decay*
> *Of that colossal wreck, boundless and bare,*
> *The lone and level sands stretch far away.*

Read into these lines imperial Spain, the Spain of Charles V, of Philip II and his Armada, the Spain of the Hapsburgs and the Bourbons; all, by the grace of time, growth, progress, by the grace of God are gone. And Philip IV, well-meaning, pleasure-loving, weak, by virtue of the arts which flourished on the decaying refuse heap of a great empire, by the penetration of a master painter's mind who served and knew him well, Philip lives on.

From the picture in the National Gallery, London
—by permission

PRINCIPAL WORKS BY VELASQUEZ

Boston, DANIELSON COLLECTION: "St. John in the Wilderness."

Boston, GARDNER COLLECTION: "Portrait of Philip IV," "Portrait of Pope Innocent IX" (attributed).

Boston, MUSEUM OF FINE ARTS: "Portrait of Don Baltasar Carlos with a Dwarf," "Portrait of a Man," "Portrait of Philip IV," "Portrait of the Infanta Maria Teresa" (attributed).

Chicago, ART INSTITUTE: "Job," "The Kitchen Maid."

Chicago, EPSTEIN COLLECTION: "Portrait of Isabel of Bourbon."

Cincinnati, MUSEUM ASSOCIATION: "Portrait of Philip IV."

Detroit, INSTITUTE OF ARTS: "Portrait of a Man."

London, NATIONAL GALLERY: "Portrait of Philip IV," "Venus and Cupid," "Christ at the Column."

London, WALLACE COLLECTION: "Portrait of a Young Girl," "Portrait of Prince Baltasar Carlos," "A Boar Hunt."

Madrid, PRADO: "The Spinners," "Las Meniñas," "The Dwarf," "The Surrender of Breda," "The Topers."

Montreal, VAN HORNE COLLECTION: "Portrait of a Young Man."

New York, FRICK COLLECTION: "Portrait of Philip IV."

New York, HISPANIC SOCIETY: "Portrait of the Count-Duke of Olivàrez," "Portrait of a Young Girl," "Portrait of Cardinal Pamphili," "Portrait of Juan de Pareja."

New York, METROPOLITAN MUSEUM OF ART: "Christ and the Pilgrims of Emmaus," "Portrait of Philip IV," "Portrait of Count Olivàrez," "Portrait of a Man."

New York, PRIVATE COLLECTIONS: Several examples.

Paris, LOUVRE: "Portrait of a Young Woman," "Portrait of Princess Margarita Maria."

Rome, DORIA GALLERY: "Portrait of Pope Innocent X."

Rutherford, N. J., WARRINGTON COLLECTION: "Angelica and Medoro."

San Francisco, CALIFORNIA PALACE OF THE LEGION OF HONOR: "Self-Portrait."

Toledo, WILLYS COLLECTION: "Portrait of a Girl."

Washington, UNITED STATES NATIONAL GALLERY OF ART: "Portrait of Pope Innocent X."

PLATE 35

MURILLO

1617-1682

The Immaculate Conception

Louvre, Paris

*

SPANISH SCHOOL

*

BARTOLOMÉ ESTÉBAN MURILLO was born at Seville of poor parents. Left an orphan at the age of ten, he was adopted by an uncle who, happily encouraging his interest in drawing pictures, eventually placed him in the studio of a local artist. Just as potential American Murillos or "inglorious Miltons" of the brush are today earning a precarious livelihood at our World's Fairs by sketching for the public, so the young Murillo occupied himself at the weekly fairs in Seville. With the little money that he could at last accumulate, he set off on foot for Madrid. He brought himself to the attention of Velasquez who, consistent with his generous nature, helped him.

After two years in the capital, Murillo, now an accomplished painter, returned to his home town. He was awarded commissions for church decorations which he executed so brilliantly as to establish himself as the foremost painter of Seville. A wealthy marriage and a circle of learned friends enhanced his prestige. He lived happily; and in the fullness of his powers at the age of 64, suffered from an accident while at work, and died.

The Immaculate Conception

By MURILLO

PIOUS and cautious by nature, and living in a period when the activities of the Inquisition were to be feared, Murillo, in the painting of religious subjects, sought and followed minutely the instructions of the authorities. His religious symbolism is the approved orthodox symbolism of his day. The details of this version of "The Immaculate Conception" are based on the verses in the Book of Revelation: "And there appeared a great sign in heaven; a woman clothed with the sun, and the moon under her feet, and upon her head a crown of twelve stars." The crown of stars, it will be noted, is omitted.

Of Murillo's versions of this subject, "The Immaculate Conception" in the Louvre is the most popular. His Madonnas were new to Spanish art; they were Andalusians "idealized" (that's the accepted term) or sentimentalized to a degree that was new in the sacred art of his country. Yet, though his world-wide reputation rests mainly upon these devotional pictures, he is perhaps to be more fairly judged by his paintings of beggars and peasants. Many of these are in the United States.

From the picture in the Louvre, Paris

PRINCIPAL WORKS BY MURILLO

Boston, MUSEUM OF FINE ARTS: "The Assumption."

Cincinnati, MUSEUM ASSOCIATION: "St. Thomas of Villanueva Dividing His Clothing Among the Beggar Boys."

Detroit, INSTITUTE OF ARTS: "The Immaculate Conception."

Glasgow, GALLERY: "The Infant St. John Playing with a Lamb."

Guadalajara, Mexico, CATHEDRAL: "Assumption of the Blessed Virgin."

Jenkintown, Pa., FISHER COLLECTION: "The Holy Family."

Kansas City, NELSON GALLERY: "The Little Conception."

London, NATIONAL GALLERY: "St. John and the Lamb," "The Holy Family."

Los Angeles, FISHER COLLECTION: "Our Lady Kneeling."

Madrid, PRADO: "The Adoration of the Shepherds," "St. John the Baptist."

Minneapolis, INSTITUTE OF ARTS: "The Pilferer Alarmed."

Montreal, VAN HORNE COLLECTION: "Portrait of a Cavalier."

New York, HISPANIC SOCIETY OF AMERICA: "St. Francis of Assisi."

New York, METROPOLITAN MUSEUM OF ART: "Portrait of Don Andres de Andrade y Col."

New York, PRIVATE COLLECTIONS: Several examples.

Pride's Crossing, Mass., FRICK COLLECTION: "Self-Portrait."

Paris, LOUVRE: "The Immaculate Conception," "The Young Beggar."

Philadelphia, PRIVATE COLLECTIONS: Some examples.

Riverside, Calif., HUTCHINGS COLLECTION: "Immaculate Conception with a Mirror."

St. Louis, CITY ART MUSEUM: "Portrait of a Man."

San Diego, MUSEUM: "Penitent Magdalen."

San Francisco, STERN COLLECTION: "A Girl with a Basket of Chickens."

Seville, CATHEDRAL: "St. Anthony of Padua Visited by the Infant Savior."

Youngstown, WARNER COLLECTION: "Madonna and Child."

PLATE 36

WATTEAU

1684-1721

Fête Champêtre

National Gallery of Scotland, Edinburgh

*

FRENCH SCHOOL

*

JEAN-ANTOINE WATTEAU was born at Valenciennes in Flanders, the son of a carpenter. Yielding to the boy's precocious talent for drawing, his father most unwillingly sent him, when fourteen, to study with an obscure local painter. To escape the importunities of his father, the boy fled to Paris where his eventual sufferings from hunger and cold laid the foundation of consumption from which, at the age of thirty-seven, he died. His drawings attracted the attention of Claude Gillot, a painter and engraver, who introduced to the young Watteau those subjects to which the pupil's own charm of imagination were to lend such lasting distinction.

Through his friendship with the great financier, Crozat, he was to enjoy for the remainder of his life that luxury to which his eyes were attuned. Wearied at last by the restraints and excitements of fashionable life, he left Crozat's friendly roof. His illness had by now so far advanced that he was beset by a depression of spirit which never left him. To seek the counsel of a noted London physician, he crossed the channel to England. He returned to France and died there.

Watteau was by nature both sensitive and wild, a product of the France of his day. He was the prototype of the school of distinguished court painters who came to record to the very moment of its tragic close an era of such reckless pleasure as no ruling class, pray God, will ever know again.

Fête Champêtre

By WATTEAU

FROM Murillo to Watteau; from the fervent unrealities which were the solace of the rulers of decaying empire, to the triumphant, light-hearted pageantry of make-believe of a court too blinded by wealth to care where wealth derived from or to think where play might lead. From Spain to France. How devastatingly does art betray its time and place, and the minds and moods and circumstances of its sponsors:

> The world's a theater, the earth a stage,
> Which God and nature do with actors fill.

The wise have known this. The French court, lacking wisdom, built for itself a theater within that larger theater, the world. And little guessing to what role in the larger drama their own acts predestined them, played on. Watteau was perhaps no wiser than the court he served, but he had eyes. And with the compelling realism of great art, he gave us in "Fête Champêtre" just what the French court was: life once too much removed.

*From the picture in the National Gallery of Scotland, Edinburgh
—by permission*

PRINCIPAL WORKS BY WATTEAU

Berlin, PALACE: "Fête Champ-être," "Departure for the Island of Cythera."

Boston, MUSEUM OF FINE ARTS: "La Perspective."

Chicago, EPSTEIN COLLECTION: "Portrait of Jean Francois Pater."

Cleveland, PRENTISS COLLECTION: "The Village Bride."

Edinburgh, NATIONAL GALLERY OF SCOTLAND: "Fête Champêtre."

London, WALLACE COLLECTION: "Return from Hunting."

New York, METROPOLITAN MUSEUM OF ART: "Le Mezzetin."

New York, PRIVATE COLLECTIONS: Several examples.

Paris, LOUVRE: "Gilles," "Jupiter and Antiope."

Philadelphia, WIDENER COLLECTION: "Woman Asleep."

Potsdam, MUSEUM: "L'Amour Paisible," "L'Enseigne de Gersaint."

PLATE 37

NATTIER

1685-1766

Portrait of Madame Sophie

Palace of Versailles

*

FRENCH SCHOOL

*

JEAN-MARC NATTIER received his first instructions in drawing and painting from his father. Although his skill in portraiture was early in evidence, his first important commission was the engraving of the Rubens' paintings in the Luxembourg Palace for Louis XIV. In 1716 he traveled to Amsterdam to paint the portrait of Peter the Great, and to the Hague where he painted the Czarina. Reduced to financial straits by a prolonged study of the Dutch masters, the repercussions of the bursting of the John Law bubble left him with no resources but his talent. He promptly turned it to account in portraiture; and winning favor from the court of Louis XV, succeeded the painter Raoux, on his death, as the favored painter of the fashionable world.

Nattier served his patrons well. To flatter his subjects had become his aim; and by the delicacy of his drawing and color he achieved it. Employing a time-honored expedient of portrait flatterers he bestowed classical divinity on his sitters, and thereby on the court itself the glory of Olympus.

Nattier outlived his vogue. He died in obscurity in 1766.

Portrait of Madame Sophie

By NATTIER

ENTIRELY in keeping with Nattier's purposeful flattery, with the general vainglory of his patrons and the particular wishfulness of the young everywhere and always, Nattier, commissioned by Louis XV to paint the portraits of the five princesses, his daughters, showed the youngest of them, Sophie,—then a schoolgirl at the Abbey Fontevrault—as the mature woman that we see.

"Madame Sophie" is Sophie-Elizabeth-Justine, fifth daughter of Louis XV and Marie Leczinska. During the period of the three youngest princesses' education at the Abbey Fontevrault, the king sent Nattier to paint their portraits as a surprise gift to their mother. The daughters of Louis XV and Marie Leczinska his queen were named Mesdames Sophie, Victoire, Louise, Adelaide, and Elizabeth. Their portraits hang at Versailles.

From the picture in the Palace of Versailles
—by permission

PRINCIPAL WORKS BY NATTIER

Boston, MUSEUM OF FINE ARTS: "Portrait of Mlle. de Bourbon-Conti."

Buffalo, CLIFTON COLLECTION: "Portrait of Mlle. de la Borde."

Cincinnati, MUSEUM ASSOCIATION: "Portrait of Mme. Thérèse de la Martinière."

Cleveland, SEVERANCE COLLECTION: "Mme. Henriette de France as Diana."

Haverford, MUCKLÉ COLLECTION: "Portrait of Henriette de Bourbon."

London, WALLACE COLLECTION: "Portrait of the Countess of Tillières."

New York, FRICK COLLECTION: "Portrait of a Lady."

New York, METROPOLITAN MUSEUM OF ART: "Portrait of the Vicomtesse de Polignac," "The Princess of Condé as Diana."

Stockholm, GALLERY: "The Duchess of Orleans as Hebe."

Versailles, PALACE: "Portrait of Marie Leczinska," "Portrait of Madame Sophie."

PLATE 38

CHARDIN

1699-1779

Le Bénédicité

Louvre, Paris

*

FRENCH SCHOOL

*

CHARDIN was born in a poor quarter of the neighborhood of the Rue de Seine, Paris, the second son of a master joiner and maker of billiard tables. His father, who had hoped that all his sons would follow in his profession, reluctantly permitted Siméon to take up art in the studio of the academician, Casus, a teacher of repute. But it was his second master, Coypel, who permitted him that freedom to pursue his own work in his own way through which he came to behold as though for the first time the immediate realities of the life around him. His paintings had an immediate popular appeal, and upon their first exhibition at the Academy elicited the praise from critics that "a new master has arisen who rivals the Dutch painters." Chardin was unanimously elected to the Academy, with the special consideration, in recognition of his poverty, of having his entrance fees reduced.

Chardin's first marriage, postponed because of his poverty, was of short duration. His wife's death left him with two children to care for. In 1744, after nine years of widowerhood, he married a widow of some substance. She cared for him tenderly until, yielding to increasing infirmities, he passed quietly away at the age of eighty years.

Le Bénédicité

By CHARDIN

WHAT the painters, Watteau, Nattier, Boucher, Fragonard, did in commemoration of the court life of their century, Chardin did for the life of that lower class which was its undercurrent. Virtually in that station into which he had been born, he lived and worked and died. In his still-lifes he has imbued the simplest and most homely objects with arresting dignity, endowing them with a warmth that was of his own kindly, generous, and simple nature. Portraits, his still-lifes might be called, of people.

And in his genre pictures he has granted to the humble people of his own class a greater dignity than to the great of France their own appointed painters would concede. And on what Chardin saw and felt—on what Chardin himself through the simple integrity of his own nature *was*—the final happiness of social man depends.

From the picture in the Louvre, Paris

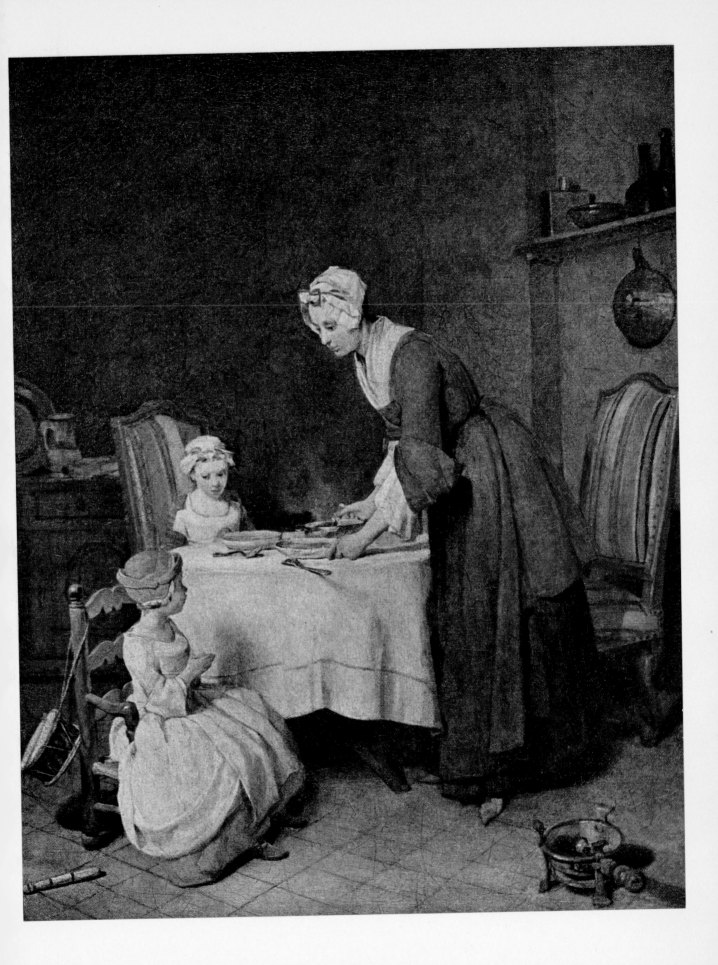

PRINCIPAL WORKS BY CHARDIN

Baltimore, MUSEUM OF ART: "Les Osselets."

Boston, MUSEUM OF FINE ARTS: "Still Life" (several).

Chicago, ART INSTITUTE: "Still Life."

Cincinnati, EDWARDS COLLECTION: "Still Life."

Dublin, NATIONAL GALLERY OF IRELAND: "Les Tours des Cartes," "The Governess."

New York, FRICK COLLECTION: "La Serinette."

New York, METROPOLITAN MUSEUM OF ART: "Supplies for Lunch," "Woman Knitting."

New York, PRIVATE COLLECTIONS: A number of examples.

Ottawa, NATIONAL GALLERY OF CANADA: "Still Life."

Paris, LOUVRE: "Le Bénédicité," "La Pourvoyeuse," "L'Enfant au Toton," "La Mère Laborieuse."

Philadelphia, JOHNSON COLLECTION: Probably the largest group of Chardin's works in the United States.

Philadelphia, PRIVATE COLLECTIONS: Several examples.

Princeton, UNIVERSITY MUSEUM: "Attributs de Peintre," "Attributs d'Architecte."

St. Louis, CITY ART MUSEUM: "Le Gobelet d'Argent."

Stockholm, NATIONAL MUSEUM: "La Toilette de Matin," "Le Bénédicité."

Vienna, LIECHTENSTEIN GALLERY: "La Gouvernante," "La Garde Attentive."

Washington, CORCORAN ART GALLERY: "Woman with a Saucepan."

Washington, PHILLIPS MEMORIAL GALLERY: "A Bowl of Plums."

Washington, UNITED STATES NATIONAL GALLERY OF ART: "Little School Mistress," "The House of Cards."

PLATE 39

BOUCHER

1703-1770

La Pompadour

National Gallery of Scotland, Edinburgh

*

FRENCH SCHOOL

*

FRANÇOIS BOUCHER was the son of an obscure "master painter." At seventeen he entered the studio of François Lemoyne where Boucher has said he had nothing to do but pass the time away. That his impressionable mind was more active than his hands is revealed by the Lemoyne influence apparent in Boucher's work. After a period of employment in the works of a maker of decorative show cards of the period, Boucher, following the custom of the French painters, visited Rome. Of the influence of Italian art the work of Boucher shows no trace. And upon his return to France he had the courage to declare that he had found Michelangelo contorted, Raphael insipid, and Correggio gloomy. The many religious pictures of his own hand [*Continued on plate 40*]

La Pompadour

By BOUCHER

JEANNE-ANTOINETTE POISSON, later to be the Marquise de Pompadour, was born in Paris in 1721. She was educated at the charge of a wealthy financier who, declaring her to be "un morceau de roi," deliberately prepared her for the high career of king's mistress. Married, presumably in preparation for her higher destiny, to a nephew of her guardian, Le Normant Etioles, (who, quite incidentally, was passionately in love with her) she promptly discarded her husband for the proffered favors of the King. Becoming at the age of twenty-three the mistress of the royal heart, she rose through the royal infatuation and her own gifts to become a dominant power in the internal politics of the realm. She was alone responsible for France's abandonment of the policy of Richelieu, which favored Germany, for that alliance with Austria which precipitated the Seven Years' War with all its disasters. She died at the age of forty-two.

From the picture in the National Gallery of Scotland, Edinburgh
—by permission

PLATE 40

BOUCHER

1703-1770

Young Lady with a Muff

Louvre, Paris

*

FRENCH SCHOOL

*

[Continued from plate 39] which he had brought back with him were acclaimed by the critics and the Academy; and, by the public and the court, ignored. It is not to be doubted that Boucher found the spirit that prevailed at the French court highly congenial to himself. At any rate, court patronage meant profit. In the sunshine of that patronage he worked; and in the light-hearted frivolity and occasional licentiousness of his subsequent work one can read a regimentation that can have been in no degree unwelcome to the artist himself. He professed to be no moralist; he was no hypocrite. The court of France played on and Boucher painted it.

Young Lady with a Muff

By BOUCHER

THE HAPPY event of Boucher's marriage at the age of thirty to the lovely seventeen-year-old Marie-Jeanne Bouseau marked the sunrise of a new day in the life of his talent. Of her beauty and great charm we know not only by the many Boucher nymphs and goddesses for which she posed, but from the unanimous tributes of her contemporaries. Their happiness together was completed by their close association in work which her own artistic gifts brought to them. Many of Boucher's paintings were reproduced by her in miniature.

The identity of the sitter for the "Young Lady with a Muff" is uncertain. Some believe her to have been the Marquise de Pompadour at a somewhat later age than in the Edinburgh portrait shown in the preceding plate.

From the picture in the Louvre, Paris

PRINCIPAL WORKS BY BOUCHER

Boston, JEFFRIES COLLECTION: "Two Figures."

Boston, MUSEUM OF FINE ARTS: "Peace and War," "L'Aller au Marché," "The Halt at the Fountain."

Chicago, ART INSTITUTE: "Bathing Nymph."

Cincinnati, EDWARDS COLLECTION: "Cupid and Venus."

Detroit, INSTITUTE OF ARTS: "The Mill at Charenton."

Edinburgh, NATIONAL GALLERY OF SCOTLAND: "Portrait of Mme. de Pompadour."

Kansas City, Missouri, NELSON GALLERY: "Jupiter and Callisto."

London, WALLACE COLLECTION: Many of his best works.

New York, FRICK COLLECTION: "The Four Seasons," "Le Dessin," "La Musique," "Portrait of Mme. Boucher," several pairs of allegorical decorations, two over-door panels.

New York, HISTORICAL SOCIETY: "Voluptuary," "Winter Scene."

New York, METROPOLITAN MUSEUM OF ART: "Birth and Triumph of Venus," "Toilet of Venus," "The Rescue of Arion from the Waves."

New York, PRIVATE COLLECTIONS: Many pieces.

Paris, LOUVRE: "Diana Leaving the Bath," "A Young Lady with a Muff."

Stockholm, NATIONAL MUSEUM: "The Triumph of Venus," "The Triumph of Galatea."

PLATE 41

PERRONEAU

1715-1783

Girl with a Cat

National Gallery, London

*

FRENCH SCHOOL

*

VERY LITTLE IS KNOWN of Perroneau's early days, but he was the son of a burgess of Paris and married a daughter of Aubert, the miniature painter. As he enjoyed but small favor at court, he worked chiefly on portraits of members of the well-to-do middle class. He was a man of unstable and roving habits, his wanderings taking him to Lyons in 1759, to Italy the same year, to Holland later on; and, in 1767, to Bordeaux, in which vicinity many of his portraits remain to this day. In 1770 he writes to his friend, Desfriches, that he finds "wandering about much cheaper than rooms in Paris, where I must live alone since the racket of children drives me mad and the stabs of the critics worry me every time." In Paris, where he was overshadowed by his great rival, de la Tour, anxieties consequent upon the dearth of patronage began the undermining of his health.

The last ten years of Perroneau's life were passed in obscurity and poverty. Restless, he returned to Holland. One day, in the year 1783, Jean Martens reported to the town clerk of Amsterdam that "The Sieur Jean-Baptiste Perroneau, of no particular profession, aged forty-two (?), living in the Heerengracht, is dead of the fever."

Girl with a Cat

By PERRONEAU

THE EIGHTEENTH century in France: The privileged dressed in satin and played at being rustics; the under-privileged toiled in poverty; and the bourgeoisie escaped reality by cultivating what may at best be termed romantic, and at its common worst sheer sentimental trash. Girl with a cat: There are three of this subject by Perroneau, and numberless others by his contemporaries.

Art can be, has been, shall be, *is* so much more than the portraying of pretty little, matron-bosomed, young lady nincompoops holding cats or anything else, that—not liking this picture a bit nor seeing, in our blindness to its values, any reason why others should like it—we make it but the occasion, in the name of art, for one brief plea to all of us: Expect great things of art. Hope to be moved by it—to happiness, to reflection; even, if need be, to sorrow. Ask very much of art. And art, great art, will answer us.

From the picture in the National Gallery, London

PRINCIPAL WORKS BY PERRONEAU

London, NATIONAL GALLERY: "Girl with a Cat."

New York, HISTORICAL SOCIETY: "Portrait of Abraham de Gallatin," "Portrait of the Wife of Abraham de Gallatin."

New York, WIMPFHEIMER COLLECTION: "Portrait of Louise, Landgräfin of Hesse."

New York, WINTHROP COLLECTION: "Portrait of Bonaventure Journu."

Ottawa, NATIONAL GALLERY OF CANADA: "Portrait of a Gentleman."

Paris, LOUVRE: "Portrait of Lambert Adam the Elder," "Portrait of Jean-Baptiste Oudry."

PLATE 42

GREUZE

1725-1805

The Broken Pitcher

Louvre, Paris

*

FRENCH SCHOOL

*

JEAN-BAPTISTE GREUZE, the son of a builder, was born in the reign of Louis XV, at Tournus, near Mâcon. Apprenticed to a painter at Lyons, he acquired a ready technique which fitted him, upon his arrival in Paris at the age of thirty, to exploit the growing need by people of substance for such concealment of the sordid realities of life as the romantic movement offered.

Greuze made immense sums of money from his paintings and from engravings after them, arousing to some degree the jealousy of his fellow Acade- [*Continued on plate 43*]

The Broken Pitcher

By JEAN-BAPTISTE GREUZE

CONCERNING the girls in Greuze's pictures, it was the opinion of the Goncourts, in part, that they show "a beauty which always has its eyes disarmed, the mouth glowing with a misty light, . . . the innocence of eighteenth-century Paris, always close to a fall." The Goncourts did not like Greuze. Camille Faust, a critic who did, considers "The Broken Pitcher" "a fine psychological bit, at once bold and subtle, which proves Greuze had a profound sensitivity to feminine expression. It is a study so strong that its science purifies its subject."

So much for critics. Of Greuze it can at least be said that his response to the patronage of the eighteenth-century upper middle class foreshadowed in kind what his spiritual descendants of nineteenth-century England were to produce at the behest of England's new industrial peerage.

From the picture in the Louvre, Paris

PLATE 43

GREUZE

1725-1805

The Milkmaid

Louvre, Paris

*

FRENCH SCHOOL

*

[*Continued from plate 42*] micians. Meanwhile the Revolution which was to terminate the era began to darken the horizon of the painter's life. When the storm broke, Greuze found himself a ruined man. At the age of seventy-six he wrote to the Minister of the Interior that he had "lost everything, even his courage and talent." He wrote the truth. It had been his fate to be born in a time of corruption and false values. Having served it well, he died at eighty, an embittered and disillusioned man.

The Milkmaid

By JEAN-BAPTISTE GREUZE

PICK the loveliest and most ethereally innocent of photographers' models; clothe her in a costume playfully designed by Schiaparelli upon the lines of a Borden milkmaid's dress, and exquisitely fashioned of imported silk; pose her with bursting bodice and a vapid saintly stare for the deft brush of the most lascivious of Academicians; call the sweet portrait "Okie," and you have a fair modern American equivalent of a Greuze.

Let—we're assuming much—such American Greuzes begin to ornament our dealers' galleries and their patrons' walls. Let—and this follows—such Greuzes be in high demand. And, with the infallibility of a Euclid solution, something to end it, as it did in France, will happen. Pray God we know in time!

From the picture in the Louvre, Paris

PLATE 44

FRAGONARD

1732-1806

The Swing

Wallace Collection, London

*

FRENCH SCHOOL

*

JEAN-HONORÉ FRAGONARD, the son of a glove maker, was born at Grasse in 1732. When he was fifteen the family moved to Paris where he was apprenticed to a notary. The skill with which he produced drawings in his spare time eventually overcame his father's objections to art as a career, and young Fragonard was placed in Chardin's studio.

In Boucher, to whom he went to study six months later, he found a spirit kindred to his own. At the age of twenty Fragonard was awarded the Prix de Rome. On his departure for Italy, Boucher said to him, "My dear Frago, you are [Continued on plate 45]

The Swing

By FRAGONARD

FROM swing to guillotine. We must realize in comparing the work of the court painters of the eighteenth century that the factual bases for their fantasies were less the creations of their own minds than of the minds of that aristocracy whose lives and interests they enlarged and glorified, and that to that aristocracy such merrymakings as are shown in Watteau's "Fête Champêtre" and in Fragonard's "The Swing" were to a large degree the very substance of what little of the reality of living their sheltered "privilege" had left them. A merry life! And who should pay for it?

That cake which the tender-hearted good queen, Marie Antoinette, proposed that the poor, lacking bread, should feed upon, could not, even to the innocence of her queen's mind, have had much frosting on it. On that frosting, if there is any significance in this tale, the queen, the king, his mistresses and courtiers lived. A bad diet for children. They were as children; it was bad for them. They died of it.

From the picture in the Wallace Collection, London
—by permission

PLATE 45

FRAGONARD

1732-1806

The Fair-Haired Boy

Wallace Collection, London

*

FRENCH SCHOOL

*

[*Continued from plate 44*] going to see Michelangelo and Raphael, but let me tell you this in friendly confidence: if you take to that kind of painting seriously, you are lost."

His life was fortunate in that enduring recognition came to him in his earlier years. At thirty-seven Fragonard married. The influence of this event upon his life is reflected in the changed nature of his subjects. Turning away from the frivolity of the court, his paintings throughout the remainder of his life are concerned with such realities as his environment presented. His work became increasingly vigorous and even realistic in character.

Despite his Republican sympathies and the intercession of his friend, the painter David, he was ousted during the turmoil of the Revolution from the studio with which the government had provided him in the Louvre. He retired with his family to Grasse. Early in the nineteenth century he returned to Paris where he died in 1806, an almost forgotten painter of a world that had meanwhile perished.

The Fair-Haired Boy

By FRAGONARD

THOUGH Fragonard continued to maintain his lucrative con-
tacts with court circles after his marriage, he tried to turn his
interest away from aristocratic frivolity to the life of his family and
home. "The Fair-Haired Boy" is a portrait of his son, Alexandre-
Évariste Fragonard.

How deeply court life colored his vision of his own family! We
do not expect an artist to paint his own son in the elegant, effeminate style which his patrons imposed upon commissioned works.
We want sincerity, directness, and honesty.

Fragonard? No, not Fragonard! The frivolous, superficial court
society of eighteenth-century France gives us as the painter's son
a pretty, elegant boy.

*From the picture in the Wallace Collection, London
—by permission*

PRINCIPAL WORKS BY FRAGONARD

Baltimore, MUSEUM OF ARTS: "Holy Family Resting."

Boston, PAINE COLLECTION: "La Bonne Mère."

Cincinnati, HANNA COLLECTION: "The Letter."

London, WALLACE COLLECTION: "Le Chiffre d'Amour," "The Swing," "The Fountain of Love," "The Schoolmistress," "The Fair-Haired Boy."

Minneapolis, INSTITUTE OF ARTS: "Astronomy."

New York, FRICK COLLECTION: "The Romance of Love and Youth" (a series).

New York, METROPOLITAN MUSEUM OF ART: "Portrait of a Lady with a Dog."

New York, PRIVATE COLLECTIONS AND SALES GALLERIES: Many examples.

Paris, BANK OF FRANCE: "La Fête de Saint-Cloud."

Paris, LOUVRE: "Corésus and Callirhoé," "The Music Lesson," "Inspiration."

Philadelphia, JOHNSON COLLECTION: "Gille — Harlequin."

San Francisco, CALIFORNIA PALACE OF THE LEGION OF HONOR: "Education of the Virgin."

San Francisco, JACKLING COLLECTION: "Portrait of Fragonard."

Washington, PHILLIPS MEMORIAL GALLERY: "Portrait of Marguerite Gerard."

Washington, UNITED STATES NATIONAL GALLERY OF ART: "Love," "Folly."

PLATE 46

LE BRUN

1755-1842

Madame Vigée Le Brun and Her Daughter

Louvre, Paris

*

FRENCH SCHOOL

*

ELIZABETH LOUISE VIGÉE, being the daughter of a portrait painter, received her first lessons from her father. She studied with the Academicians Briard and Doyen, was helped to some extent by Greuze, and conducted her studies in the studio of the painter Le Brun, whom she married. Le Brun's dissipated habits made the marriage intolerable. She left him.

In 1783, having already won as a painter the favor of the court, she was welcomed to the Academy. In her own list of her own paintings are included all of the better known figures in court and in Parisian society. She maintained a salon that was one of the most elegant and lively in Paris.

During the heat of the Revolution, and being through her court associations out of sympathy with it, she left France to reside for periods in Rome, Parma, Venice, Vienna and, for six years, in St. Petersburg. Shortly after her return to Paris in 1801, she again went to England, remaining there for three years. She died at the advanced age of eighty-seven.

Madame Vigée Le Brun and Her Daughter

By LE BRUN

WITHOUT even mentioning her daughter's name, Madame Le Brun, in her memoirs, relates how that daughter fell in love with "a certain Nigris." Despite the mother's objections to the marriage, she obtained the consent of her estranged husband. "The cruel child" remained ungrateful. After the wedding Madame Le Brun called on the bride in her new home. M. Nigris, she relates, was bundled in a great Russian overcoat, coddling a cold. While Nigris was occupied in conversation with another visitor, the mother inquired after her daughter's happiness. "I confess," pouted the young lady, "that that fur coat is disenchanting; how could you expect me to be smitten with such a figure as that?"

Madame Le Brun, as the testimony of her contemporaries and her own art show her to have been, was one of the most attractive of the cultivated and charming personalities of the arts who served the court and aristocracy of that doomed regime and era, late eighteenth-century France. That many were involved in its fall was severe justice to be visited upon good souls whose hearts—for artist's hearts are good—were better than their minds. It was the good fortune of Madame Le Brun that she suffered little more than inconvenience.

From the picture in the Louvre, Paris

PRINCIPAL WORKS BY LE BRUN

Baltimore, DUGAS COLLECTION: "Portrait of Mme. Dugas de Vallon."

Detroit, WHITCOMB COLLECTION: "Portrait of Marie Antoinette."

London, NATIONAL GALLERY: "Self-Portrait."

Minneapolis, INSTITUTE OF ARTS: "Portrait of Giovanni Paesiello."

New York, METROPOLITAN MUSEUM OF ART: "Young Girl with Flowers."

Paris, LOUVRE: "The Artist and Her Daughter" (two versions), "Peace Bringing back Plenty."

Philadelphia, WANAMAKER COLLECTION: "Portrait of Madame Elizabeth de France."

Silver Spring, Md., McCORMICK-GOODHART COLLECTION: "Portrait of Marie Antoinette."

Versailles, PALACE: "Portrait of Marie Antoinette and Her Children."

PLATE 47

COROT

1796-1875

Souvenir de Mortefontaine

Louvre, Paris

*

BARBIZON SCHOOL

*

IT WAS VERY reluctantly that Jean-Baptiste-Camille Corot's father, a fashionable milliner, permitted him to adopt painting as a career. It was the usual story: the world of commerce offered greater opportunity. But finally the Corot parents settled a small income on their son and let him have his way. Being able to travel, study, and paint without having to sell pictures, Corot had a free artistic development. Society made no demands. Up to his fiftieth year he painted in a social vacuum. He could not have existed on the proceeds of the sale of his pictures, for buyers were few and far between.

Suddenly Corot adopted a new style. The new development of photography fascinated him. Quickly he took up its point of view. This was the sort of painting his contemporaries liked, and beginning about the year 1850 they bought and bought and bought. Corot turned out pictures by the hundreds. They flooded homes and museums and public places, and were specially favored by American buyers.

He died in 1875, a wealthy man, highly respected by his contemporaries. He had gained more of fame and fortune than a career of his father's choosing might ever have brought him.

Souvenir de Mortefontaine

By COROT

HERE is but one of the many popular landscapes that Corot turned out prolifically and repetitiously, all with the same gray, wispy tonality, formless foliage, and monotonous composition. There was an eager market for these paintings. They made Corot rich, brought him fame and prestige. The painting of the last years of his life contributed nothing to his artistic reputation. Critics today do not approve of this portion of his works. Looking back to the magnificent work of his early years, comparing this landscape with a canvas like "The Port of La Rochelle," we cannot help regretting that so much of Corot's genius pandered to the public taste and patronage that were always ready in the nineteenth century to applaud and purchase pictures painted down to an exceedingly low level of appreciation.

Corot did not always paint in this fashion. A few years ago a New York gallery acquired an early canvas, bold and clear, bathed in brilliant light. It was placed on the wall without a legend; and visitors were asked to guess. Nine out of ten attributed it to a twentieth-century painter. Some placed it in the school of Cubism!

From the picture in the Louvre, Paris

Bethlehem, Pa., EUGENE GRACE COLLECTION: "Twilight."

Boston, MUSEUM OF FINE ARTS: "Ville d'Avray" and others, comprising probably the largest Corot collection in the United States.

Brooklyn, INSTITUTE: "An Italian Girl."

Chicago, ART INSTITUTE: "The Bridge of Trysts" and several others.

Cincinnati, MUSEUM ASSOCIATION: "Le Lac," "Don Quixote."

Cincinnati, TAFT MUSEUM INSTITUTE OF FINE ARTS: "The Heights of Ville d'Avray," "Les Baigneuses à l'Enfant," "Souvenir of Riba — Evening Glory."

Cleveland, MUSEUM OF ART: "The Willows."

Columbus, Ind., IRWIN COLLECTION: "The Leaning Tree at the Fish Pond."

Des Moines, WEEKS COLLECTION: "A Young Woman in a Red Bodice."

Detroit, FORD COLLECTION: "Edge of the Pool."

Hartford, WADSWORTH ATHENEUM: "Landscape," "Rouen from the Hill of St. Catherine," "Landscape with Figure."

Kansas City, Mo., NELSON GALLERY OF ART: "Italian Scene — View of Subiaco," "Les Villes au Pin Parasol."

Los Angeles, MABURY COLLECTION: "Limay, near Mantes — the Seine and the Old Bridge."

Merion, Pa., BARNES FOUNDATION: "Girl Seated."

Minneapolis, INSTITUTE OF ARTS: "A Village Square."

Montreal, ART ASSOCIATION: "L'Île Heureuse," "The Willow Walk."

Muskegon, Mich., HACKLEY ART GALLERY: "L'Étang aux Villas," and others.

New York, FRICK COLLECTION: "Le Matin — Lac de Garde," "Ville d'Avray," "L'Étang," "Le Lac."

New York, METROPOLITAN MUSEUM OF ART: One of the largest Corot collections in the United States.

Northampton, Mass., SMITH COLLEGE MUSEUM OF ART: "Town on a Cliff," "Jumièges," "The Spring," "La Blonde Gasconne."

Paris, LOUVRE: "The Belfry of Douai," "Souvenir de Mortefontaine," "Portrait of Mme. Baudot," "A Lady with a Pearl Necklace."

Philadelphia, PENNSYLVANIA MUSEUM OF ART: "Gipsy Woman at the Fountain."

Providence, METCALF COLLECTION: "Le Marais."

Providence, RHODE ISLAND SCHOOL OF DESIGN: "Edge of a River, Hills in the Distance."

Reims, MUSEUM: "View of Nantes."

St. Louis, MALLINCKRODT COLLECTION: "Le Pecheur."

St. Paul, HILL ESTATE: "Eurydice Blessée," "Le Printemps de la Vie," "La Peche au Filet."

San Francisco, CALIFORNIA PALACE OF THE LEGION OF HONOR: "Bridge of the Castel Sant' Angelo."

Springfield, Mass., MUSEUM OF ARTS: "Vue de Naples."

Washington, CORCORAN GALLERY: "Ronde de Nymphes."

Washington, PHILLIPS MEMORIAL GALLERY: "La Grande Métairie," "Portrait de Femme," "Woman with Water Jar."

Washington, UNITED STATES NATIONAL GALLERY OF ART: "Une Idylle Ronde," "Le Lac de Garde."

Wellesley, Mass., FARNSWORTH MUSEUM: "Inn at Montigny-les-Cormeilles."

PLATE 48

MILLET

1814-1875

The Angelus

Louvre, Paris

*

BARBIZON SCHOOL

*

JEAN-FRANÇOIS MILLET was born on the land and spent his boyhood working his father's fields. His early drawings came to the attention of a local painter at Cherbourg who accepted him as a pupil. The municipality granted him a small annual pension which permitted him to continue his studies in Paris.

The official system of training in Paris, at the École des Beaux Arts, was too inflexible for Millet's temperament. He could not get along with his teachers and decided to work alone. He earned his daily bread turning out hack portraits and bad copies.

Painters in his time had a way of banding together in self-defense. A small group of men—Diaz and Rousseau among them—were attracted by Millet's work. They softened the blow caused by the death of his first wife and urged him to continue the struggle.

In 1848 "The Winnower" was very well received by the public and at last found Millet a patron. Then, on the proceeds of this sale and a few commissions, he purchased a small house at Barbizon, on the outskirts of Fontainebleau. Here for twenty-seven years he continued to paint his simple story of peasant life, quietly, with great dignity.

By 1860 he was financially secure and enjoyed until he died the peace which he so directly and simply expressed in his painting.

The Angelus

By MILLET

MANY of Millet's contemporaries painted simple folk and simple things. None possessed the dignity and sincerity with which he approaches a subject such as this. These peasants were his own people. In his youth he had plowed the land by their side. His memory retained their attitudes and gestures. He pictured them, as he did here, without sentimentality or false idealism.

The deep sincerity and transparent honesty which breathe in "The Angelus" have attracted to it a constant and deserved popularity. People who work with their hands have not often been well treated by painters. At times they are ridiculed; frequently they are pictured in forced gayety, away from their work. To Millet must go the credit of painting the laborer with the feeling that best fits the subject: dignity.

From the picture in the Louvre, Paris

PRINCIPAL WORKS BY MILLET

Baltimore, WALTERS COLLECTION: "Baigneuse," "The Potato Diggers," "Breaking Flax."

Boston, MUSEUM OF FINE ARTS: "The Sower," "The Potato Planters," "Self-Portrait," "Girl Spinning," "Homestead at Gréville," "The Reapers," and others.

Boston, PRIVATE COLLECTIONS: Many examples.

Cambridge, FOGG ART MUSEUM: "Girl with Sheep," "Shepherds Resting."

Chicago, ART INSTITUTE: "Sheep Shearers," "Bringing Home the New-Born Calf," "Woman Feeding Chickens," "Rail Splitter," and others.

Cincinnati, MUSEUM ASSOCIATION: "Going to Work."

Cincinnati, TAFT COLLECTION INSTITUTE OF FINE ARTS: "Mother and Child."

Cleveland, BURKE COLLECTION: "Sheep Shearing."

Copenhagen, CARLSBERG GLYPTOTHEK: "Death and the Woodcutter."

Kansas City, NELSON GALLERY: "L'Attente."

New York, FRICK COLLECTION: "Woman and Lamp."

New York, METROPOLITAN MUSEUM OF ART: "Autumn," "Garden Scene," "Woman with a Rake."

New York, PRIVATE COLLECTIONS AND SALES GALLERIES: Many examples.

Northampton, SMITH COLLEGE MUSEUM OF ART: "The Farm at Gréville."

Ottawa, NATIONAL GALLERY OF CANADA: "Oedipus Taken Down from the Tree."

Paris, LOUVRE: "The Gleaners," "The Angelus."

Philadelphia, JOHNSON COLLECTION: "Marine."

Philadelphia, PENNSYLVANIA MUSEUM OF ART: "The Pig Killers."

Saint Paul, HILL ESTATE: "Woman Spinning."

San Francisco, MUSEUM OF ART: "The Man with the Hoe."

Toledo, MUSEUM OF ART: "Quarriers," "Gleaner."

PLATE 49

MEISSONIER

1813-1891

"1814"

Louvre, Paris

*

FRENCH SCHOOL

*

MEISSONIER—SUPER-ACADEMICIAN—succeeded with a vengeance. Had his father anticipated only mildly the glory and wealth that were to come to his son, he might not have been so hostile to the profession of painting. But Meissonier had the urge badly and ultimately convinced his father. He was a good student and learned his craft well. Fortunately for him, he had a mind that did not soar above the mediocrity of his contemporaries. He was a hard worker, and loved to achieve perfection in small details. His observation of nature was scrupulous and impeccable, and his style was well adapted to "official" painting.

Fame came to Meissonier and so did riches—as they should come to perseverant, industrious men who fit well and comfortably into an established scheme of things.

"1814"

By MEISSONIER

SINCE historical documentation is this canvas' only excuse
for being, it is important to point out that this is not the re-
treat from Moscow. Napoleon and his staff are returning from
Soissons after the battle of Laon. And this is very probably just
what they looked like that day. Meissonier, true to form, went to
unbelievable trouble to make certain that each square inch of
canvas be true to detail. He was thorough to an extreme; to him
research was the backbone and sinew of art. That is what makes
reproduction of his work so valuable in textbooks of history. We
have seen this painting so frequently reproduced in our school-
books that it is conceivable that Meissonier's conception of Napoleon is the basis of a popular fancy that people in institutions,
suffering from delusions of grandeur, inevitably stand all day with
their right hand clutching at their hearts through the second and
third buttons of their jackets.

From the picture in the Louvre, Paris

PRINCIPAL WORKS BY MEISSONIER

Baltimore, WALTERS COLLECTION: "Napoleon – 1814."

Boston, AMES ESTATE: "The Stirrup Cup."

Hartford, WADSWORTH ATHENEUM: "Man Reading."

London, WALLACE COLLECTION: "Halt at the Inn," "The Print Collectors," "The Roadside Inn," "The Decameron."

New York, METROPOLITAN MUSEUM OF ART: "Friedland, 1807," "The Lute Players," "The Sign Painter," "The General and His Aide-de-Camp," "The Brothers Van de Velde."

New York, WINTHROP COLLECTION: "Bacchus."

Paris, LOUVRE: "1814."

Paris, LUXEMBOURG: "Napoleon III at Solferino."

Philadelphia, PENNSYLVANIA ACADEMY OF FINE ARTS: "Cavalier Awaiting an Audience."

PLATE 50

MUENIER

1863-1934

The Music Lesson

Luxembourg, Paris

*

FRENCH SCHOOL

*

JULES-ALEXIS MUENIER was born in 1863 in the Haute-Saône district to the south of Paris. The middle-class milieu of his early life provided the material for the subject matter of the greater part of his painting. It was in this field that he practised his art for more than forty years until the first showing of "The Catechism Lesson" in the Paris Salon of 1909 brought him notable success. His technique and point of view were derived from his study and training with the painter Dagnan-Bouveret, whose religious subjects became enormously popular in France after 1880. Muenier's late life was distinguished by an intimate friendship with Marshal Foch and his portrait of the general is the likeness best known to most of us. In his last years Muenier became exclusively a painter of portraits.

The Music Lesson

By MUENIER

As NEWER comers crowd the fore
We drop behind—
We who have laboured long and sore
Times out of mind,
And keen are yet, must not regret
To drop behind.

"The Music Lesson" was exhibited at the Paris Salon of 1912 and was purchased immediately by the French government. The sweet, charming proximity of youth to old age is a subject widely represented in academic painting, for it produces inevitably an emotional response that warms a sentimental heart.

From the picture in the Luxembourg, Paris

PRINCIPAL WORKS BY MUENIER

Paris, THE LUXEMBOURG: "The Music Lesson."

Mulhouse, MUSEUM: "The Orphans," "Bathers."

There are none of Muenier's well-known works in public galleries in the United States.

PLATE 51

MANET

1832 - 1883

The Bar at the Folies-Bergères

Courtauld Institute of Art, London

*

IMPRESSIONIST SCHOOL

*

EDOUARD MANET was one of the great masters of French painting. He was the son of a magistrate and began life as a cabin-boy, starting early the habit of travel which was later to influence his manner of painting. He studied for a short time with Couture. Visits to Holland and Spain brought him into direct contact with the work of Velasquez and Hals whose brushwork became his model.

In 1863, Manet was brought violently to public attention by the bitter controversy which arose after the exhibition of his famous "Déjeuner sur l'Herbe." The picture represents a group of men and women having a picnic in the woods; the women are only partly clothed. A stultified public could not easily stomach so simple a subject treated in monumental terms. Again, in 1865, Manet had a *succès de scandale,* the "Olympia," a nude in everyday surroundings, unromanticized, unsweetened. Public hostility this time was so intense that Manet, discouraged and heartbroken, traveled to Spain.

When he returned the so-called school of Impressionism was practically established. Manet became identified with this group—Monet, Sisley, Pissarro, Renoir, and Degas—but never went very far ahead in experimentation. In 1883 he died without enjoying the benefits of his mastery.

The Bar at the Folies-Bergères

By MANET

IN THE roaring twenties, when the market boomed and paper wealth was abundant in the land, American tourists, weary of Main Street or Broadway, put on their best tweed knickers and betook themselves to Paris where life was free and wild and gay. There was one thing in Paris which few of us ever overlooked: The Folies-Bergères. The French were shrewd; this was made specially for us—the opulence, the nudity, the daring. And we loved it. We came back and took our friends into corners, poked our elbows into their ribs, and told them surreptitiously of the wonders we had seen. Really, we thought, French culture had it all over ours. *They* knew how to do things. And they weren't slaves to inhibitions. That was the Paris of the twenties.

Here, in Manet's picture, is the Paris of the 1880's, the Folies-Bergères of his day. Just a night club, without a special reputation; a place where actors, writers, business men, doctors, lawyers, even painters, went of an evening to relax, hear a popular song or two, dance a while, drink a little, then go home to sleep. Manet was there often with his friends. He liked it, and so he painted it.

But the public of his times couldn't get the point. Despite the lovely color and splendid composition, they were antagonistic. Why? For the same reason so much good painting in the nineteenth century was neglected or abused. The subject, people thought, was beneath the dignity of art!

From the picture in the Courtauld Institute of Art, London
—by permission

PRINCIPAL WORKS BY MANET

Boston, GARDNER COLLECTION: "Portrait of His Mother."

Boston, MUSEUM OF FINE ARTS: "Monk in Prayer."

Boston, PRIVATE COLLECTIONS: Several examples.

Chicago, ART INSTITUTE: "Jesus Mocked by the Soldiers," "Sortie du Porte de Boulogne," "Race Course at Longchamps," "Bull Fight," "The Philosopher," "A Beggar," "Le Journal Illustré."

Cincinnati, EDWARDS COLLECTION: "Still Life."

Detroit, TANNAHILL COLLECTION: "Women on the Beach."

Hillsboro, California, CROCKER COLLECTION: "The Grand Canal, Venice."

Honolulu, ACADEMY OF ARTS: "A Negress."

Kansas City, NELSON GALLERY: "Portrait of Line Campineanu."

London, COURTAULD INSTITUTE OF ART: "The Bar at the Folies-Bergères."

London, TATE GALLERY: "La Servante de Bocks," "Portrait of Mlle. Eva Gonzales."

Merion, Pa., BARNES FOUNDATION: "Le Linge."

New Orleans, HUNT COLLECTION: "Vases of Flowers."

New Orleans, HENDERSON COLLECTION: "Portrait of Berthe Morisot."

New York, FRICK COLLECTION: "Bull Fight."

New York, METROPOLITAN MUSEUM OF ART: "Dead Christ with Angels," "Boy with a Sword," "The Funeral," "Woman with a Parrot," "Jean," "En Bateau," "Barque de Dante," "Torero Saluting," "Mlle. Victorine in the Costume of an Espada."

New York, PRIVATE COLLECTIONS AND SALES GALLERIES: Several examples.

Paris, LOUVRE: "Olympia," "Le Déjeuner sur l'Herbe," "Le Fifre," "Le Balcon."

Philadelphia, PRIVATE COLLECTIONS: Several examples.

St. Louis, CITY ART MUSEUM: "Le Leseur."

Toledo, MUSEUM OF ART: "Portrait of Antonin Proust."

Washington, DUMBARTON OAKS COLLECTION: "The Spanish Dancers."

Washington, PHILLIPS MEMORIAL GALLERY: "Marine."

Washington, UNITED STATES NATIONAL GALLERY OF ART: "Boy with a Sword."

PLATE 52

CÉZANNE

1839-1906

Chestnut Trees at Jas de Bouffan

Frick Collection, New York

*

POST-IMPRESSIONIST SCHOOL

*

IT WAS FORTUNATE for modern art (of course, for Cézanne) that his father was a banker who was persuaded to permit Cézanne to study and paint without the worry of having to sell his pictures.

Paul Cézanne was born at Aix where he was the schoolmate of Émile Zola. The two boys decided early to practise the arts. Zola left home for Paris soon after finishing school. Cézanne, after a few spasmodic attempts at following his father's footsteps, settled at the capital, where he became known as one of the most vehement of the revolutionary painters. After 1870 an association with the Impressionist Pissarro brought to him a new point of view that was to modify and redirect his artistic life. He did not stop at Impressionism but learned from its technique a new method and a new aim, a preoccupation with form that was later to be the obsessional drive behind his work.

Cézanne spent the last two decades of his life at Aix, with his wife and family, in a painstaking and perseverant effort to solve the problems of painting form through color. The world of art knew nothing of his important progress and scarcely remembered his name. In 1904 there was held at Paris a retrospective exhibit of Cézanne's painting. It was then, two years before his death, that France suddenly awakened to his genius.

Chestnut Trees
at Jas de Bouffan

By CÉZANNE

CÉZANNE sometimes spent years working on a single picture. Some of his portrait subjects had to sit through more than one hundred long sessions, only to hear him say, "Too bad, it won't turn out. Better forget about it." And the picture would be left unfinished, or cut into shreds, or thrown into a garbage barrel.

The mountains of Provence, which Cézanne painted time and time again, were more perfect subjects. They could better stand the tedium of endless posing, and their appearance did not change from day to day—an important consideration for a painter like Cézanne.

The blue peak seen behind the complicated weaving of bare branches is Mont Sainte-Victoire. Cézanne painted it hundreds of times; close up, in a long view, from the front, from the back, from both sides.

In the discussion of most painting it is not necessary to get involved in technical difficulties. Appreciation does not require it. Cézanne, though, was consciously and deliberately solving technical problems in all of his painting. Since this landscape is a fine example of what he was trying to accomplish, a brief excursion into the technical aspect of his painting should not seem either artificial or superfluous. He wanted to reduce form to simple and clear existence through the architectural use of color. He broke up the surface of his pictures into separate independent areas of color which, in total effect, build up to an appearance of solidity. You will see this clearly if you examine the foreground of this landscape.

From the picture in the Frick Collection, New York

PRINCIPAL WORKS BY CÉZANNE

Beverly Hills, Calif., EDWARD G. ROBINSON COLLECTION: "Still Life with a Clock."

Burlington, Vt., WINTERBOTHAM COLLECTION: "Apples."

Chestnut Hill, Mass., PAINE COLLECTION: "Self-Portrait," "Portrait of Mme. Cézanne."

Chicago, ART INSTITUTE: "The Bay from L'Estaque," "La Corbeille de Pommes," "Pistachio Tree," and many others.

Chicago, McCORMICK COLLECTION: "The Bathers."

Detroit, FORD COLLECTION: "Still Life."

Detroit, TANNAHILL COLLECTION: "Portrait of Mme. Cézanne."

Hollywood, Calif., ARENSBERG COLLECTION: "The Bathers."

London, TATE GALLERY: "Bathers," "Rocky Landscape."

Merion, Pa., BARNES FOUNDATION: "Still Life," "View of Gardanne," "Mont Ste.-Victoire," "Les Grandes Baigneuses," "The Bathers," "The Drinker."

Montreal, VAN HORNE COLLECTION: "Portrait of Mme. Cézanne."

Moscow, MUSEUM OF MODERN WESTERN ART: An extensive collection, too numerous to itemize.

New Rochelle, N. Y., MILLER COLLECTION: "The Bathers."

New York, FRICK COLLECTION: "Chestnut Trees at Jas de Bouffan."

New York, METROPOLITAN MUSEUM OF ART: An extensive collection, too numerous to itemize.

New York, MUSEUM OF MODERN ART: Probably the most extensive collection in the United States of Cézanne's works.

New York, PRIVATE COLLECTIONS: Many specimens.

Northampton, Mass., SMITH COLLEGE MUSEUM OF ART: "The Road that Turns."

Paris, LOUVRE: "Les Joueurs de Cartes," "La Maison du Pendu."

Philadelphia, PENNSYLVANIA MUSEUM OF ART: "Mont Ste.-Victoire."

St. Louis, CITY ART MUSEUM: "Mlle. Marie Cézanne."

Santa Barbara, Calif., CLARK COLLECTION: "Nature Morte au Pichet."

Washington, PHILLIPS MEMORIAL GALLERY: "Self-Portrait."

PLATE 53

RENOIR

1841-1919

La Loge

Courtauld Institute of Art, London

*

IMPRESSIONIST SCHOOL

*

FIRMIN-AUGUSTE RENOIR, son of a tailor, was born at Limoges, center of the French porcelain industry. At the age of four he was taken to Paris with his family. At school his music teacher was the composer, Gounod, who urged upon him a career in music. But the Renoirs were poor, and it was a help to them when Auguste, at the age of thirteen, was apprenticed to a porcelain painter. During his lunch hours he ran from the pretty little flowers on cups and saucers to the Louvre where he hastily copied old masters. A few years later Renoir progressed from teapots to delicate fans, and finally, at twenty, he entered the studio of Gleyre.

For twelve years he had a terrible struggle keeping alive, painting pictures in exchange for food, shelter, and clothing. In 1875 he painted portraits of the Charpentier family, and thereafter, under its benevolent protection, enjoyed a modicum of financial success.

Renoir was a born painter who loved nothing more in life than the play of his brush upon canvas. There are more than five thousand of his pictures in existence. Even in old age, in Provence, where he settled late in life, he continued to paint with a brush strapped to his arm after arthritis and rheumatism had deadened his hands. Of him it may truly be said that he died painting.

La Loge

By RENOIR

THIS canvas isolates a fragment of Parisian life of Renoir's time. It is an unimportant fragment, of no special significance, just a man and woman sitting in a box at the opera. Renoir was a spontaneous painter, direct and effervescent. His love of the intrinsic act of painting, of applying pigment to a surface, is evident in everything that has come from his hand. This surface is luminous and rich; it appeals even to the sense of touch, and almost invites a caress. To a painter like Renoir subject matter was unimportant; color, design, and surface were his chief interests.

The gentleman peering through his glasses is believed to be Renoir's brother. His charming companion was Renoir's favorite model. Her full and robust charm is more directly exhibited in hundreds of his other canvases.

It was this picture, exhibited at the famous Impressionist Exhibition of 1874, that first brought Renoir into the limelight. Actually it did not belong with the canvases with which it was hung. For Renoir, though he sympathized with the aims of the Impressionist school, never adopted its methods or technical practices.

From the picture in the Courtauld Institute of Art, London
—by permission

Beverly Hills, Calif., ROBINSON COLLECTION: "Place de la Trinité," "After the Bath."

Boston, MUSEUM OF FINE ARTS: "The Seine at Chatou," "On the Grand Canal, Venice."

Boston, PRIVATE COLLECTIONS: Many examples.

Burlington, Vt., WINTERBOTHAM COLLECTION: "Young Girl."

Cambridge, FOGG ART MUSEUM: "At the Milliner's."

Chicago, ART INSTITUTE: "Fruits of the Midi," "Chrysanthemums," "Picking Flowers," and many others.

Cincinnati, EDWARDS COLLECTION: "The Little Algerian."

Cleveland, COE COLLECTION: "Flowers in a Jar," "Promenade au Bord de la Mer," "Trois Baigneuses au Crabe," "Portrait of Mme. Sert."

Detroit, INSTITUTE OF ARTS: "Graziella."

Detroit, PRIVATE COLLECTIONS: Some examples.

Hollywood, LAUGHTON COLLECTION: "The Judgment of Paris."

London, COURTAULD INSTITUTE OF ART: "La Loge."

London, NATIONAL GALLERY: "Umbrellas."

Merion, Pa., BARNES FOUNDATION: "The Spring" (two versions), "Pasture near the Seine," and more than thirty others.

Minneapolis, INSTITUTE OF ART: "Battledore and Shuttlecock."

Moscow, MUSEUM OF MODERN WESTERN ART: "La Grenouillière," "Reverie," "Portrait of a Lady in Black," and others.

Naugatuck, Conn., WHITTEMORE COLLECTION: "The Duck Pond," "Girl with a Cat."

New Orleans, HENDERSON COLLECTION: "Still Life – Melon and Flowers," "Tulips," and others.

New York, FRICK COLLECTION: "Mother and Children."

New York, METROPOLITAN MUSEUM OF ART: "Au Bord de la Mer," "La Famille Charpentier."

New York, MUSEUM OF MODERN ART: "Landscape."

New York, PRIVATE COLLECTIONS AND SALES GALLERIES: Many examples.

Northampton, SMITH COLLEGE MUSEUM: "Portrait of Mme. Edouard Maître."

Nyack, N. Y., HAYES COLLECTION: "Girl in a Lace Hat."

Paris, LOUVRE: "Le Moulin de la Galette," "Portrait of Mme. Charpentier," "Bathers."

Paris, LUXEMBOURG: "The Reader."

Philadelphia, PENNSYLVANIA MUSEUM OF ARTS: "Portrait of Mme. Renoir."

Philadelphia, PRIVATE COLLECTIONS: Several examples.

Providence, RHODE ISLAND SCHOOL OF DESIGN: "Young Man Reading an Illustrated Journal."

Roxbury, Va., CHAMBERS COLLECTION: "Paysage," "Child with Book."

St. Louis, CITY ART MUSEUM: "Portrait of the Artist's Father," "La Songeuse."

San Francisco, CROCKER COLLECTION: "Still Life with Flowers and Prickly Pear."

Toledo, MUSEUM OF ART: "The Green Jardinière."

Toronto, ART GALLERY: "The Seine at Chatou," "Portrait of Claude."

Washington, PHILLIPS MEMORIAL GALLERY: "The Canoeists at Lunch."

PLATE 54

VAN GOGH

1852-1890

Sun Flowers

Tate Gallery, London

*

POST-IMPRESSIONIST SCHOOL

*

PEOPLE TODAY KNOW more about Van Gogh's life than his painting. It was a strange life, by common standards; full of impulses, frustrations, and revolt.

Vincent Van Gogh was employed first by a firm of picture dealers, but could not adjust himself to the procedures and the routine of a commercial career. Then his missionary bent took him to the coal fields of Belgium where he became a lay preacher. Here, as in all things, he showed too much enthusiasm; his impulses were too direct, too sincere. The miners did not understand or welcome his zeal.

Van Gogh had always taken to drawing for amusement. At this time he began to draw and paint, not so much for personal pleasure, but more in terms of a professional career. He went to the south of France—to Arles—where he loved the sun and the warm rich colors of Provence. It was a difficult struggle, a life of poverty and want. Despite the hardship, Vincent's production was enormous; he [Continued on plate 55]

Sun Flowers

By VAN GOGH

THOUGH Van Gogh's style was a very personal one, it neverthe-less was forcefully influenced by Impressionism and by his ad-miration of Japanese painting. From the Impressionists he bor-rowed his palette—intense, clean pigments. Before his contact with the Impressionist school, his colors had been dark and muddy, following the contemporary style of his native Holland. From Japa-nese painting (see the background of his "Self-Portrait") he took the method of what is known technically as "line and flat tone"—using broad, unrelieved areas of flat color without attempting to model surfaces.

This still-life demonstrates clearly Van Gogh's practice of ap-plying pigments in ribbons, at times directly from the tube. This technique gives his work a suggestion of violent motion which at times becomes so exaggerated that it destroys the total effect of a picture.

*From the picture in the Tate Gallery, London
—by permission*

PLATE 55

VAN GOGH

1852-1890

Self-Portrait

Courtauld Institute of Art, London

*

POST-IMPRESSIONIST SCHOOL

*

[*Continued from plate 54*] painted wildly, almost palpably as the result of that inner drive which had pushed him past so many frustrations and which had by now, as the result of so much disappointment and defeat, begun to derange his brain. He was, in the popular sense of the word, a lunatic, and was interned for a short time in an asylum. He lived for the most part alone, for he could not get along with people. His friendship with the painter, Gauguin, did not endure; while it lasted it was interrupted frequently by violent quarrels and outbursts of uncontrolled temper.

Toward the end his fits of madness came more frequently; in lucid moments he was bogged down by profound melancholy. Despite the kindness and sympathy of his brother, Theo, and the understanding of Dr. Gachet, an admirer and true friend, the struggle proved too much for him. In 1890 he destroyed his own life.

Self-Portrait

By VAN GOGH

IN HIS last years at Arles, when his mind was going rapidly to pieces, Van Gogh was in the habit of paying visits to one of Arles' less reputable brothels. Its inmates knew him as a "peculiar" man and often made jokes at his expense. Poor Vincent—he took all things seriously. And so, one day, he saw nothing facetious in the remarks of one of the girls who suggested jokingly that she might be delighted some day to receive one of his ears as a present. Promptly he amputated his ear and gave it to her.

This is a self-portrait which exhibits the painful result of that ludicrous episode. Vincent's eyes are sad and melancholy. He is acknowledging here that he is a defeated man, neither understanding the world nor understood by it.

*From the picture in the Courtauld Institute of Art, London
—by permission*

PRINCIPAL WORKS BY VAN GOGH

Boston, MUSEUM OF FINE ARTS: "Postman (Le Facteur Roulin)."

Boston, PRIVATE COLLECTIONS: Several examples.

Burlington, Vt., WINTERBOTHAM COLLECTION: "The Drinkers," "Self-Portrait."

Chicago, ART INSTITUTE: "Van Gogh's Bedroom at Arles," "Still Life," "Soleil du Midi – Arles," "Montmartre," "La Berceuse (Madame Roulin)."

Detroit, INSTITUTE OF ARTS: "Self-Portrait in a Straw Hat."

Glasgow, MACINNES COLLECTION: "Le Moulin de la Galette."

Kansas City, NELSON GALLERY: "Olive Grove."

London, COURTAULD INSTITUTE: "Self-Portrait."

London, TATE GALLERY: "Sunflowers," "Landscape with Cypress Trees," "The Chair."

Moscow, MUSEUM OF MODERN WESTERN ART: "Shrubs," "Landscape at Auvers, after the Rain," "Cottages at Auvers,"

"The Red Vineyard of Arles," "Marine," "La Ronde des Prisonniers," "Portrait of Dr. Rey," "Promenade à Arles."

New York, METROPOLITAN MUSEUM OF ART: "Landscape."

New York, PRIVATE COLLECTIONS AND SALES GALLERIES: A great many excellent examples, notably "L'Arlésienne" in the Adolf Lewisohn Collection.

Paris, LOUVRE: "La Guingette," "Restaurant de la Sirène."

Philadelphia, JOHNSON COLLECTION: "A Vase of Flowers."

Philadelphia, TYSON COLLECTION: "Sunflowers."

Providence, DANFORTH COLLECTION: "Restaurant at Arles."

St. Louis, CITY ART MUSEUM: "Stairway at Auvers."

Toledo, MUSEUM OF ART: "Houses at Auvers," "Le Champ de Blé."

Washington, PHILLIPS MEMORIAL GALLERY: "The Garden of Arles."

PLATE 56

HOGARTH

1697-1764

The Shrimp Girl

National Gallery, London

*

EARLY BRITISH SCHOOL

*

WILLIAM HOGARTH, born in London on November 10, 1697, was the son of Richard Hogarth, a schoolmaster and literary hack. The boy showed little aptitude for learning from school books but compensated for this by the delight and energy with which he ornamented their margins. He was accordingly apprenticed to a silverplate engraver; and here he learned that craft, engraving, which, applied to copper, was to serve him all his life. He has written, "Engraving on copper was, at twenty years of age, my utmost ambition."

Having eloped with the only daughter of Sir James Thornhill, sergeant-painter to the king, he married her. Two years later, Hogarth completed the earliest of that series of moral works, "A Harlot's Progress," which was to establish him as an original genius of satire.

In 1757 he succeeded his father-in-law, John Thornhill, as sergeant-painter to the king. At the age of sixty-five he became involved in an unfortunate public quarrel which, while it produced two of his keenest and most devastating minor satires, the portraits of his one-time friends, John Wilkes and the poet Churchill, doubtless contributed to that general collapse of health which terminated with his death.

The Shrimp Girl

By HOGARTH

TO HOGARTH the brush and the engraver's burin were to be used, as is the writer's pen, for the expression of ideas. Preeminently a close and critical observer of life, he served art less than art was made to serve his social consciousness. The very fierceness of his satire of the human animal reveals him as having been far less aware of human dignity, or moved by it, than stirred to hatred of those social forces of his time in London which were destroying it. What man had made of man, he loathed. He fought it bitterly.

Horace Walpole who, incidentally, disliked him, said, "Hogarth's pictures are the most faithful criticism on our way of life that we have had in a hundred years." Constantly criticized and attacked by artists—who found what Hogarth did not to be art—he met with wide favor from the public. Posterity has found that public to have been right.

"The Shrimp Girl" is not characteristic of the volume of Hogarth's work by which he is known. It may reveal to us the heart that beat behind his social satires. The subject is unquestionably one of that large and noisy profession of hawkers who, purveying everything from rat traps to salvation, infested the streets of seventeenth-century London. Doubtless she cried her shrimp as in the streets of Londonderry sweet Molly Malone cried "Cockles and mussels alive, alive O!"

From the picture in the National Gallery, London
—by permission

Boston, MUSEUM OF FINE ARTS: "Portrait of the Countess Kingston with Her Son," "Portrait of Earl Kingston and His Son."

Chicago, ART INSTITUTE: "Monamy and Walker."

Cold Spring Harbor, L. I., JENNINGS COLLECTION: "Portrait of Governor Thomas Hutchinson."

Detroit, INSTITUTE OF ARTS: "Portrait of a Lady."

London, FOUNDLING HOSPITAL: "Portrait of Captain Thomas Coram."

London, NATIONAL GALLERY: "Marriage à la Mode," "Self-Portrait," "Calais Gate," "The Shrimp Girl."

London, NATIONAL PORTRAIT GALLERY: "Portrait of Simon Fraser," "Portrait of Lord Lovat," "Meeting of a Committee of the House of Commons."

London, SOANE MUSEUM: "The Rake's Progress," "The Election."

Manchester, Mass., COOLIDGE COLLECTION: "Portrait of a Woman."

Muskegon, Mich., HACKLEY GALLERY: "Portrait of Anne, Viscountess Irwin."

New York, FRICK COLLECTION: "Portrait of Miss Mary Edwards."

New York, METROPOLITAN MUSEUM OF ART: "Portrait of Peg Woffington," "The Price Family," "The Jeffreys Family," "The Wedding of Mr. Stephen Beckingham and Miss Mary Cox of Kidderminster."

New York, PRIVATE COLLECTIONS: Several examples.

Ottawa, NATIONAL GALLERY OF CANADA: "Portrait of John Herring, Esq."

Philadelphia, PRIVATE COLLECTIONS: Several examples.

Pride's Crossing, Mass., FRICK COLLECTION: "Portrait of the Hon. John Hamilton."

Providence, RHODE ISLAND SCHOOL OF DESIGN: "The Ballad Singer."

St. Louis, CITY ART MUSEUM: "Lord and Lady Grey as Children."

San Marino, HUNTINGTON COLLECTION: "Portrait of Frederick Meinhart Frankland."

Washington, CORCORAN GALLERY: "Portrait of a Woman."

Washington, SMITHSONIAN INSTITUTION NATIONAL COLLECTION OF FINE ARTS: "Portrait of Mrs. Price."

PLATE 57

REYNOLDS

1723-1792

The Age of Innocence

National Gallery, London

*

EARLY BRITISH SCHOOL

*

JOSHUA REYNOLDS was born at Plymton near Plymouth in 1723. He was a gifted and precocious child and at the age of fifteen, having developed a passion for the works of Raphael, informed his father that he wished to be a painter. Sent to London to study, he became a pupil of Thomas Hudson, a well-known portrait painter. His acquaintanceship with the painter, William Godey, whose father had been a pupil of Van Dyck, was of some importance in the development of Reynolds' talent.

At the age of twenty-six he visited Italy. He was less impressed by the Raphael of his boyhood enthusiasm than by the Venetian painters. They were to have a lasting influence upon Reynolds' style. Reynolds' success, measured by recognition, was immediate and lasting. He was the unquestioned leader of the English school of his day. He founded the Society of British Artists; and when in 1768 this society became the Royal Academy, Reynolds was elected president and knighted. As president of the Royal Academy he exemplifies in its finest sense the Academic in thought and in achievement. Reynolds was an indefatigable worker. He had a well-balanced mind, was honorable in the conduct of his life, generous in his attitude toward the younger artists, and in the best sense a polished and accomplished gentleman.

The Age of Innocence

By REYNOLDS

IN THE time of Reynolds there lived in England an eccentric engraver, painter, and writer of mystical poems, one William Blake. Neglected by his contemporaries, he is recognized today as one of the great original geniuses of mankind.

On the margins of his copy of Reynolds' "Discourses" he supplied in his own hand a running commentary. On page two of the first "Discourse" this appears: "I consider Reynolds' 'Discourses to the Royal Academy' as the Simulations of the Hypocrite who smiles particularly when he means to Betray. His praise of Rafael is like the Hysteric Smile of Revenge. His Softness and Candour, the hidden trap and the poisoned feast. He praises Michel Angelo for Qualities which Michel Angelo abhorr'd, and he blames Rafael for the only qualities which Rafael Valued. Whether Reynolds knew what he was doing is nothing to me; the Mischief is just the same whether a Man does it Ignorantly or Knowingly. I always consider'd True Art & True Artists to be particularly Insulted and Degraded by the Reputation of these Discourses, As much as they were Degraded by the Reputation of Reynolds' Paintings, & that Such Artists as Reynolds are at all times Hired by the Satans for the Depression of Art—a Pretence of Art, To destroy Art."

From the picture in the National Gallery, London
—by permission

Albany, INSTITUTE AND HISTORICAL AND ART SOCIETY: "Portrait of Sir John Hamilton."

Alexandria, Va., MASONIC LODGE: "Portrait of the Sixth Lord Fairfax."

Atlanta, HIGH MUSEUM: "Portrait of Richard Brinsley Sheridan."

Baltimore, MUSEUM OF ART: "Portrait of the Duke and Duchess of Marlborough."

Baltimore, PEABODY INSTITUTE: "Self-Portrait."

Berkeley, Calif., CLARK COLLECTION: "Portrait of Lady Charlotte Johnstone," "Portrait of Frederick, Duke of York."

Boston, MUSEUM OF FINE ARTS: Several portraits.

Brooklyn, MUSEUM: "Portrait of Christopher Baek."

Chicago, ART INSTITUTE: "Portrait of Lady Sarah Bunbury."

Cincinnati, TAFT COLLECTION INSTITUTE OF FINE ARTS: Portraits.

Cleveland, MUSEUM OF ART: "Mrs. Collier as Lesbia."

Detroit, INSTITUTE OF ARTS: "Portrait of Mrs. Chalmers," "Portrait of Sir Brooke Boothby."

Elmira, ARNOT GALLERY: "Portrait of Miss Hanna Vincent."

Greenwich, SIMMONS COLLECTION: "Portrait of Thomas Bowlby."

Indianapolis, TARKINGTON COLLECTION: "Portrait of Mary, Countess of Rothes."

Kansas City, NELSON GALLERY: "Portrait of George Ashby."

London, NATIONAL GALLERY: "Portrait of Lord Heathfield," "Lady Cockburn and Her Children," "The Graces Decorating a Figure of Hymen."

London, NATIONAL PORTRAIT GALLERY: "Portrait of Anne Seymour Damer."

London, WALLACE COLLECTION: "Portrait of Nelly O'Brien,"

New York, FRICK COLLECTION: "Portrait of Lady Skipwith," "Portrait of Elizabeth, Lady Taylor."

New York, METROPOLITAN MUSEUM OF ART: "Portrait of Sir Edward Hughes," "Portrait of Mrs. Arnold," "Portrait of Lady Carew," and others.

New York, PUBLIC LIBRARY: "Mrs. Billington as St. Cecilia," "Portrait of Miss Kitty Fisher."

Ottawa, NATIONAL GALLERY OF CANADA: "Venus in a Landscape," "Portrait of Jeffrey Lord Amherst," "Portrait of Colonel Charles Churchill."

Philadelphia, MUSEUM OF ART: "Portrait of Master Bunbury."

Pittsburgh, CARNEGIE INSTITUTE: "Portrait of Mrs. Dawkins."

Pride's Crossing, Mass., FRICK COLLECTION: "Portrait of Sir George Howland Beaumont," "Portrait of Margaret, Lady Beaumont," "Portrait of Lady Cecil Rice."

Providence, ATHENAEUM: "Portrait of Miss Theophila Brown."

St. Louis, JAMISON COLLECTION: "Portrait of Miss Mary Church."

San Marino, HUNTINGTON COLLECTION: "Mrs. Siddons as the Tragic Muse," "The Holy Family," and others.

Toledo, MUSEUM OF ART: "Portrait of Mrs. Watson."

Washington, CORCORAN GALLERY: "Portrait of Isabelle d'Amida."

Washington, SMITHSONIAN INSTITUTION NATIONAL COLLECTION OF FINE ARTS: Portraits.

Washington, UNITED STATES NATIONAL GALLERY OF ART: "Lady Betty Delme and Her Children," "Portrait of Lady Elizabeth Compton," "Portrait of Lady Caroline Howard."

Worcester, ART MUSEUM: "Madonna and Child," "Portrait of Captain Bligh."

PLATE 58

GAINSBOROUGH

1727-1788

Portrait of Mrs. Siddons

National Gallery, London

*

EARLY BRITISH SCHOOL

*

THOMAS GAINSBOROUGH was born at Sudbury in Suffolk, one of a large family of children. He showed precocious interest in painting and drawing. At the age of twelve when his father refused him a letter that would procure him a day off from school, he forged such a letter and spent the day sketching in the woods. The indignant father exclaimed, "Tom will be hanged!" Then, seeing the sketches: "No, he will be a genius." Few fathers are so wise.

At fourteen he was sent to London where he studied art—first with a French engraver, then with a bad painter of historical pictures. Returning at eighteen to Sudbury, he married; and with a wife endowed with the considerable income of £200 a year, he moved to Ipswich. Though portrait commissions constituted at this time [Continued on plate 59]

Portrait of Mrs. Siddons

By GAINSBOROUGH

SARAH KEMBLE SIDDONS, the eldest of twelve children of Roger Kemble, was born in a public house at Brecon, Wales, in 1755. At the age of eighteen she married William Siddons.

Her first important impression on the stage was made at Cheltenham in Artway's "Venice Preserved." The people of "quality" who came to laugh, departed in tears. Garrick, hearing of her success, employed her to appear at Drury Lane at a salary of five pounds a week. Her greatest triumph was as Isabella in Garrick's version of Southerne's "Fatal Marriage." Mrs. Siddons' most famed role was Lady Macbeth, to the tragedy of which her stature, her shining beauty, and the dignity of her demeanor lent moving power. Mrs. Siddons had the friendship and respect of her most eminent contemporaries. And Dr. Johnson, as a dramatic gesture of homage, inscribed his name on the hem of her garment in that portrait of her by Reynolds in which she appears as the "Tragic Muse."

Mrs. Siddons died in London in 1831.

From the picture in the National Gallery, London
—by permission

Ardmore, Pa., STOUT COLLECTION: "Portrait of Lord Vernon."

Bethlehem, Pa., GRACE COLLECTION: "Crossing the Stream."

Boston, MUSEUM OF FINE ARTS: "Portrait of John Eld," "Portrait of Mrs. Edmund Morton Pleydell," "The Blind Man on the Bridge," "Portrait of the Artist's Daughter."

Cambridge, FOGG ART MUSEUM: "Portrait of Benjamin Thompson, Count Rumford."

Chicago, ART INSTITUTE: "Valley of the Avon," "Landscape with Figures and Cattle," "Portrait of the Countess of Bristol."

Cincinnati, ART MUSEUM: "Portrait of Viscount Downe," "Portrait of Anne Ford."

Cincinnati, INSTITUTE OF FINE ARTS: "Portrait of Sir Francis Bassett, Lord de Dunstanville," "Portrait of Maria Walpole, Duchess of Gloucester," "Portrait of Edward and William Tomkinson."

Cincinnati, PRIVATE COLLECTIONS: Several examples.

Cleveland, PRENTISS COLLECTION: "Pastoral Landscape," "Portrait of the Hon. Mrs. Wise."

Detroit, INSTITUTE OF ARTS: "Portrait of Mrs. Mead."

Detroit, SMITH COLLECTION: "Portrait of Mrs. David Garrick."

Edinburgh, NATIONAL GALLERY: "Portrait of the Hon. Mrs. Graham."

Hartford, WADSWORTH ATHENEUM: "The Broken Egg."

Kansas City, JONES COLLECTION: "The Market Cart."

Kansas City, NELSON GALLERY: "Repose."

London, NATIONAL GALLERY: "Portrait of Mrs. Siddons," "The Market Cart," "Portrait of Dr. Ralph Schomberg."

London, NATIONAL PORTRAIT GALLERY: "Portrait of Charles, Marquess Cornwallis."

London, TATE GALLERY: "The Watering Place," "Portrait of Edward Orpen."

London, WALLACE COLLECTION: "Portrait of Miss Haverfield."

Manchester, Mass., COOLIDGE COLLECTION: "Portrait of Mr. Hood."

Montreal, ART ASSOCIATION: "Rustic Courtship."

Muskegon, HACKLEY COLLECTION: "Portrait of William Lynch."

New York, FRICK COLLECTION: "Landscape," "Portrait of the Hon. Annie Duncan," "Portrait of Lady Inness," "Portrait of Mrs. Hatchett," "The Mall," and others.

New York, METROPOLITAN MUSEUM OF ART: "Child with a Cat," "Portrait of the Rev. Humphrey Burroughs," "Portrait of a Man," "Landscape," "English Landscape."

New York, PRIVATE COLLECTIONS AND SALES GALLERIES: Many examples.

New York, PUBLIC LIBRARY: "Romantic Woody Landscape."

Ottawa, NATIONAL GALLERY OF CANADA: "Portrait of Ignatius Sancho."

Philadelphia, PENNSYLVANIA MUSEUM OF ART: "Portrait of Mrs. Tudway," "Portrait of Mrs. Richard Brinsley Sheridan."

Piqua, Ohio, FLESH COLLECTION: "Portrait of Thomas Sheridan."

Pittsburgh, BYERS ESTATE: "Portrait of Mrs. David Kinloch."

Pittsburgh, JONES COLLECTION: "Portrait of William Yelverton Davenport," "The Cottage Door," "Portrait of Miss Hobson," "Portrait of William Pitt."

[*Continued*]

PLATE 59

GAINSBOROUGH

1727-1788

The Blue Boy

Huntington Collection, San Marino, California

*

EARLY BRITISH SCHOOL

*

[*Continued from plate 58*] his chief support beyond the income of his wife, he grew restive. "I am tired of portraits," he said. "I would like to take my Viol-de-gamba and go and live in some peaceful village where I could paint landscapes and enjoy the last period of my life in tranquility and well-being, but these fine ladies with their cups of tea, their balls, their husband-hunting, cheat me out of my last years."

Gainsborough was one of the charter members of the Royal Academy. Unlike his distinguished rival, Reynolds, Gainsborough, instinctive and emotional, was little inclined to intellectual activity. No reasoner himself, he had respect for the intelligence of others. In apology for a lack of deference he feared he might have shown Reynolds, he wrote: "Dear Sir Joshua: I write today to tell you from a sincere heart that I have always sincerely loved and admired Sir Joshua Reynolds."

The Blue Boy

By GAINSBOROUGH

IT WAS the published opinion of the theorizing Sir Joshua Reynolds that blue, being a "cold" color, could not serve as the central color mass in a well-planned picture. Tradition relates that "The Blue Boy" was painted as a deliberate challenge to Reynolds' theory. If price may be held a criterion of intrinsic worth, Gainsborough's "The Blue Boy," which in recent years was bought for the Huntington Collection in California for the price of $750,000, may be said to have proved Reynolds wrong. But price is no criterion. And as far as the pleasant anecdote is concerned, "The Blue Boy" happens to have been painted eight years before the publication of Reynolds' statement. "The Blue Boy" is a portrait of Master Jonathan Buttall.

The picture, *and* its cash value, have been so highly and successfully publicized that, without fear of contradiction, we may pronounce the painting to be one of the half dozen most popular pictures of the world. It is, nevertheless, a good picture.

From the picture in the Huntington Collection, San Marino, California

PRINCIPAL WORKS BY GAINSBOROUGH

(*Continued*)

Pittsburgh, R. B. MELLON COLLECTION: "Portrait of the Rt. Hon. William Pitt, Chancellor of the Exchequer."

Rochester, N. Y., UNIVERSITY: "Portrait of Mrs. Provis."

Rye, N. Y., PRICE COLLECTION: "The Cart," "Portrait of Isabella, Countess of Dundonald."

St. Louis, CITY ART MUSEUM: "View in Suffolk."

St. Louis, PRIVATE COLLECTIONS: Some examples.

San Marino, HUNTINGTON COLLECTION: "The Blue Boy," "The Cottage Door," "Portrait of Viscount Ligonier," and several others.

Toledo, MUSEUM OF ART: "Portrait of Lady Frederick Cambell."

Toledo, SECAR COLLECTION: "Coast Scene."

Villa Nova, Pa., MONTGOMERY COLLECTION: "A View in Shropshire."

Washington, CORCORAN GALLERY: "Portrait of Frances, Lady de Dunstanville," "Portrait of Lord de Dunstanville."

Washington, SMITHSONIAN INSTITUTION NATIONAL COLLECTION OF FINE ARTS: "Portrait of Lord Mulgrave in Naval Uniform."

Washington, UNITED STATES NATIONAL GALLERY OF ART: "A Family at the Cottage Door," "Landscape with a Bridge," "View on the English Coast with Boats and Figure," and many portraits.

Washington, WALKER COLLECTION: "Portrait of the Artist's Father."

PLATE 60

ROMNEY

1734-1802

The Parson's Daughter

National Gallery, London

*

EARLY BRITISH SCHOOL

*

GEORGE ROMNEY was born at Dalton-in-Furness, Lancashire, on December 26, 1734, the son of a builder and cabinet maker. Manifesting a gift for mechanics, the boy was instructed in that craft; and the carving of figures in wood being part of the instruction, he made a violin. Then, having made it, he took to playing it.

At nineteen George was apprenticed to an itinerant portrait painter. Three years later he fell ill of fever. Through the devoted ministrations of Mary Abbott, the young daughter of his landlady, the fever was at last driven from his body, only to enter and possess his heart. He cured himself of that: he married her. And six years later, to advance his own career and shed the encumbrance of a rustic wife, he left her and went to London. But for a few occasional visits during the course of his life he never saw her again until, at the age of sixty-five, suffering from growing weakness of body and depression of mind, he returned to his still faithful and devoted wife. Throughout his three remaining years she nursed him tenderly.

The Parson's Daughter

By ROMNEY

ART which should be, and at its greatest is, a medium for the expression of *all* that a man through all his faculties perceives, and comes to know of life, was to the brush of Romney—as it has been to all who through their work achieve the full expression of themselves—no less than just exactly that. The trouble with Romney lies in his having been no more, in character, in mind, in quality or depth of heart, than a lightly emotional and sensitive, impulsive, unreflecting man. Profound emotion will engender thought; and thought, that disciplining of the mind which leads to order and conviction, was as alien to Romney's nature as was the disciplining of his life for the discharge of his responsibilities and the accomplishment of his purposes. Romney just couldn't think; he lightly, tenderly, and sweetly felt.

And of "The Parson's Daughter"—whoever she may have been—he tells of nothing but her youthful charm. And history tells less.

From the picture in the National Gallery, London
—by permission

Boston, MUSEUM OF FINE ARTS: "Mrs. Billington as St. Cecilia," "Portrait of James Fenton," and other portraits.

Brooklyn, MUSEUM: "Portrait of Miss Mingay," "Portrait of Mrs. Fenton."

Bryn Mawr, Pa., COLES COLLECTION: "Portrait of Mrs. Tickell."

Chicago, ART INSTITUTE: "Portrait of Mrs. Francis Russell."

Cincinnati, MUSEUM ASSOCIATION: "Mrs. Corbet and Her Daughter."

Cincinnati, PRIVATE COLLECTIONS: Several examples.

Cincinnati, TAFT COLLECTION INSTITUTE OF FINE ARTS: "Portrait of Mrs. John Johnson."

Cleveland, MUSEUM OF ART: "Portrait of Lady Reid."

Columbus, Ohio, SCHUMACHER COLLECTION: "Portrait of Miss Robinson."

Grosse Pointe, Mich., NEWBERY COLLECTION: "Portrait of a Young Man."

Haverford, Pa., ELY COLLECTION: "Portrait of Richard Brinsley Sheridan," "Portrait of a Gentleman with a Red Coat," "Portrait of Col. John Penn."

Kansas City, NELSON GALLERY: "Portrait of Lord Fernham."

London, NATIONAL GALLERY: "The Parson's Daughter," "Portrait of Lady Hamilton," and others.

London, WALLACE COLLECTION: "Mrs. Robinson as Perdita."

Manchester, Mass., COOLIDGE COLLECTION: "Portrait of Lady Jane Hope."

Montreal, ANGUS COLLECTION: "Portrait of Mrs. Wright."

New York, FRICK COLLECTION: "Lady Hamilton as Nature," "The Countess of Warwick and Her Children," "Portrait of Lady Milnes," "Portrait of Miss Mary Finch-Hatton."

New York, METROPOLITAN MUSEUM OF ART: "Lady Hamilton as Daphne," "Portrait of Mrs. Fitzherbert," "Self-portrait," and others.

New York, PRIVATE COLLECTIONS: Many examples.

Ottawa, NATIONAL GALLERY OF CANADA: "Portrait of Thayandanegea (Joseph Brant)."

Philadelphia, MUSEUM OF ART: "Portrait of Mrs. Tickell," and others.

Philadelphia, PENNSYLVANIA MUSEUM OF ART: "The Willett Children," "Little Bo-Peep," and others.

Philadelphia, PRIVATE COLLECTIONS: Many examples.

Pittsburgh, CARNEGIE INSTITUTE: "Portrait of John Mills."

Pittsburgh, PRIVATE COLLECTIONS: Many examples.

Rye, N. Y., PRICE COLLECTION: "Portrait of Lady Wedderburn."

San Marino, HUNTINGTON COLLECTION: "Portrait of Caroline, Viscountess Clefden, and Her Sister," and many other portraits.

Toledo, MUSEUM OF ART: "Portrait of Lord McLeod."

Toronto, ART GALLERY: "Portrait of Henry James Richter, Esq."

Villa Nova, Pa., MONTGOMERY COLLECTION: "Portrait of Mr. Bethune."

Washington, SMITHSONIAN INSTITUTION NATIONAL COLLECTION OF FINE ARTS: "Portrait of Miss Kirkpatrick," "Portrait of Sir Sampson Wright."

Washington, PRIVATE COLLECTIONS: Several examples.

PLATE 61

RAEBURN

1756-1823

A Boy with a Rabbit

Diploma Gallery, London

*

EARLY BRITISH SCHOOL

*

HENRY RAEBURN was born at Stockbridge, a suburb of Edinburgh, on March 4, 1756. He was left an orphan at the age of nine and placed in school in Edinburgh. In school he showed no particular talents or inclinations although, through strict attention to his school exercises, he acquired in the six years that he remained at school an education that was sufficient for his subsequent intercourse with the men of letters of his day. Upon leaving school at the age of fifteen, he chose to follow the industrial art of a goldsmith. It may be that the manual dexterity which his work as a goldsmith's assistant developed proved of some value in his subsequent career. It was at least of service in his early practice of the art of miniature painting in which he began to take an interest. Raeburn served his employer Gilliland faithfully; and Gilliland in return allowed young Raeburn all possible freedom for miniature painting. Raeburn's skill increased and through the interest of his generous employer he began securing commissions.

Of Raeburn a biographer has written, "The motions of the artist were as regular as those of a clock. In summer he rose at seven, took breakfast at eight with his wife and child, walked up to his great room in York Place, and was ready for a sitter by nine." Raeburn died at the age of 67.

A Boy with a Rabbit

By RAEBURN

"A BOY WITH A RABBIT" in England; "Girl with a Cat" (Plate 41) in France; both, and their pretty kind, too much and everywhere in eighteenth-century Europe to augur well for those and all their class who liked them. Let us not be led so far astray by our conditioned penchant for the sentimental as an avenue of escape from the actualities of life as to abandon common sense when confronted by art. "A Boy with a Rabbit": its title is the statement of its whole intention. Judge it by that. Is this young manhood as we'd have it? Give us—for we Americans must have our say—one page of "Huckleberry Finn" for all the Raeburn boys on earth. Give us, oh Henry Varnum Poor (American, c. today), one "Boy with Woodchuck"—or with Coyote, Gopher, Porcupine, or nothing at all—and, looking at it we'll have renewed faith that "a government of the people, by the people, and for the people shall not perish from the earth."

From the picture in the Diploma Gallery, Burlington House, London
—by permission

Baltimore, YOUNG COLLECTION: "Portrait of Lord Cockburn."

Boston, MUSEUM OF FINE ARTS: "Portrait of Lord Hope," "Portrait of Robert Hay."

Cincinnati, MUSEUM ASSOCIATION: "The Elphinstone Children."

Cincinnati, TAFT COLLECTION INSTITUTE OF FINE ARTS: Portraits.

Cleveland, EATON COLLECTION: "Portrait of Mr. Clark of Montrose."

Concord, N. H., WINANT COLLECTION: "Portrait of Sir David McKie."

Detroit, FISHER COLLECTION: "Portrait of Mrs. Grant of Kilgraston."

Detroit, INSTITUTE OF ARTS: "Portrait of the Hon. Henry Erskine," "Portrait of the Hon. Henry David Erskine, Earl of Buchan."

Edinburgh, NATIONAL GALLERY OF SCOTLAND: "Portrait of Miss Scott Moncrieff," "Portrait of Col. Macdonnell of Glengarry."

Glasgow, CORPORATION ART GALLERY: "Portrait of William Mills, Provost of Glasgow."

Greenwich, Conn., SIMMONS COLLECTION: "Portrait of Dr. James Gregory," "Portrait of General McKenzie of Monzie."

Hartford, WADSWORTH ATHENEUM: "Portrait of Peter Van Brugh Livingston."

Haverford, Pa., ELY COLLECTION: "Portrait of a Scottish Gentleman."

Indianapolis, TARKINGTON COLLECTION: "Portrait of Mrs. Urquhart."

Kansas City, NELSON GALLERY: "Portrait of Master Alexander McKenzie," "Portrait of Sir George Abercrombie," "Portrait of Lady Abercrombie."

London, DIPLOMA GALLERY, BURLINGTON HOUSE: "A Boy with a Rabbit."

London, NATIONAL GALLERY: "Portrait of Lt. Col. Bryce MacMurdo," "Portrait of a Lady."

London, NATIONAL PORTRAIT GALLERY: "Portrait of Henry Mackenzie," "Portrait of the Rt. Hon. Sir John Sinclair."

New York, METROPOLITAN MUSEUM OF ART: "Portrait of Mrs. James Gilchrist," "Portrait of Dr. Black," and others.

New York, PUBLIC LIBRARY: "Portrait of Lady Bellhaven," "Portrait of Peter Van Brugh Livingston."

Philadelphia, MUSEUM OF ART: "Portrait of Alexander Shaw," "Portrait of Master Thomas Bisland."

Piqua, Ohio, FLESH COLLECTION: "Portrait of John Campbell of Kilberry."

Pittsburgh, CARNEGIE INSTITUTE: "Portrait of Thomas Miller of Edinburgh."

Pride's Crossing, Mass., FRICK COLLECTION: "Portrait of Alexander Allan."

Providence, DANFORTH COLLECTION: "Portrait of Robert Sim."

St. Louis, WASHINGTON UNIVERSITY: "Portrait of Mrs. Halkett."

San Marino, HUNTINGTON COLLECTION: Several portraits.

Washington, CORCORAN GALLERY: "Portrait of Mrs. Vere of Stonebyres."

Washington, SMITHSONIAN INSTITUTION NATIONAL COLLECTION OF FINE ARTS: "Portrait of a Man," "Portrait of Archibald Skirving."

Washington, UNITED STATES NATIONAL GALLERY OF ART: "John Tait and His Grandson John Tait," and other portraits.

Worcester, ART MUSEUM: "Portrait of Mrs. Rennie Strachan."

Youngstown, WARNER COLLECTION: "Portrait of James Byres of Tonley," "Portrait of Col. Francis James Scott."

PLATE 62

MORLAND

1763-1804

Interior of a Stable

National Gallery, London

*

EARLY BRITISH SCHOOL

*

GEORGE MORLAND was the son of an artist. At the age of fifteen he was exhibiting at the Royal Academy. His father was a hard taskmaster; so, finding home unbearable, young Morland escaped to Margate where his talents earned him enough to live in comfort and indulge and cultivate his growing taste for drink. Back in his native London, he married, at the age of 23, Maria Ward, and for a few months showed signs of reforming. His work, which recalls to a small degree some of the old Flemish painters, was immensely popular, and his colored engravings are to be found in innumerable homes throughout England. He lived extravagantly and kept as many as a dozen horses. He accumulated debts, and to escape his creditors, he moved from one hiding place to another, in and out of London, followed wherever possible by his devoted wife.

From a brief respite on the Isle of Wight, he returned to London where he spent the remaining years of his life exploring the legal possibilities open to a debtor who was broke. The debtors' prison, "letters of license," and the sponging-house were tried in turn, until, still painting desperately in an effort to meet his obligations, he died, at the early age of forty-one.

Interior of a Stable

By MORLAND

A GREAT deal of art criticism today stems from Freud—and frequently ends with Freud. The psychological, or psycho-analytic, approach to appreciation is, in certain instances, a very effective instrument. For when certain paintings seem to us to have not enough artistic merit to warrant extended discussion, and yet remain popular pictures liked by common people, we had better turn to the subject matter and try to discover just why the painter chose it and why people react to it favorably.

Morland was a wastrel, a congenital drunkard. He practised none of the homely virtues.

Here he warmly paints horses and a stable. It is a scene that praises simple labor, a good life close to the earth, industry and kindness. This is what the psychologists call "compensation"—expressing artistically or otherwise what we lack internally and fail to practise. Morland's fondness for a subject such as this had perhaps the same motivation that prompts us—how ridiculously—to isolate seven days a year for "Be Kind to Animals Week" when well we know that this idea of concentrating a virtue temporarily betrays the truth that we are not gentle in our treatment of living things as a general rule.

From the picture in the National Gallery, London
—by permission

Bryn Mawr, Pa., RADFORD COLLECTION: "Contentment."

Cincinnati, TAFT COLLECTION INSTITUTE OF FINE ARTS: "Gathering Apples."

Hartford, WADSWORTH ATHENEUM: "On the Road to the Derby."

Kansas City, NELSON GALLERY: "The Wreck, Isle of Wight."

Lexington, Ky., WIDENER COLLECTION: "Sportsman Relieving a Poor Family."

London, GILBEY COLLECTION: "Gypsies in a Wood," "The Dipping-Well," "The Deserter's Farewell."

London, NATIONAL GALLERY: "The Interior of a Stable," "Clover Field with Figures," "Rabbiting."

London, VICTORIA AND ALBERT MUSEUM: "Lansdown Fair."

New York, HISTORICAL SOCIETY: "Dogs Fighting," "Old English Sportsman."

New York, METROPOLITAN MUSEUM OF ART: "Midday Meal," "The Bell Inn," "Landscape with Figures."

New York, PRIVATE COLLECTIONS: Some examples.

New York, PUBLIC LIBRARY: "Pigs in a Fodder Yard," "Marine View — Isle of Wight."

Ottawa, NATIONAL GALLERY OF CANADA: "Wreckers."

Philadelphia, MUSEUM OF ART: "Old Coaching Days," "The Cottager's Family."

Philadelphia, PENNSYLVANIA MUSEUM OF ART: "The Fruits of Early Industry and Economy."

Philadelphia, PRIVATE COLLECTIONS: Several examples.

Pride's Crossing, Mass., FRICK COLLECTION: "Interior of a Stable."

Rye, N. Y., PRICE COLLECTION: "Landscape with Bridge and Figures."

Silver Spring, Md., McCORMICK-GOODHART COLLECTION: "Seascape."

Toronto, WOOD COLLECTION: "Rural Gossips."

Villa Nova, Pa., MONTGOMERY COLLECTION: "Hounds Casting off Near the Gamecock Inn."

Washington, CORCORAN GALLERY: "Farmhouse."

Washington, PARMELEE COLLECTION: "Woodcutters."

White Plains, N. Y., HILL COLLECTION: "Smugglers."

Worcester, ART MUSEUM: "Farmyard Scene."

Yonkers, BOYCE THOMPSON COLLECTION: "The Old Man's Story."

PLATE 63

LAWRENCE

1769-1830

Portrait of Master Lambton

The Earl of Durham's Collection, Lambton Castle, County Durham

*

EARLY BRITISH SCHOOL

*

THOMAS LAWRENCE was born in 1769, the son of an unsuccessful man of many trades. During his father's incumbency of the Black Inn at Devizes the boy, besides entertaining his father's customers by reciting to them, drew their portraits in chalk. Later, at Bath, at that time a center of fashionable society, the crayon portraits of the boy Lawrence had a vogue at the price of ten to fifteen dollars each.

At about the age of eighteen, Lawrence went to London, taking a portrait of himself to Sir Joshua Reynolds for his advice. "You have been looking too much at the Old Masters, I see," said Reynolds, "and my advice is: study nature." Lawrence entered as a student at the Royal Academy Schools.

At the age of twenty-one Lawrence came into fame, and a year later he was elected an associate of the Academy. Upon Reynolds' death in the [Continued on plate 64]

Portrait of Master Lambton

By LAWRENCE

CHARLES WILLIAM LAMBTON: He was born in 1818. He
sat for Lawrence's portrait at about the age of six; and at the
age of thirteen, he died. Of the popularity of the picture those of
us who carry memories of Victorian homes need not be reminded.
Although the picture hangs in a private collection in England, it
is known, and has been loved, over all the western world through
the colored mezzotints, engravings and other reproductions that
have been published. And when, in 1932, it was put up for sale an
offer of £95,000 was refused. If we *must* judge a picture, if we are
determined to arrive at a definite evaluation of it as art, there is a
factor—a fourth dimension, let us say—that must be considered:
that factor, or dimension, is Time. And Time (the Period in which
we live) is a factor in that the very faculties by which we judge
have been conditioned by it. Little Charles William Lambton:
people of Byron's England loved to believe that boys were just like
that. And Lawrence helped them.

From the picture in the Earl of Durham's collection
—by permission

Baltimore, PRIVATE COLLECTIONS: Many portraits, often of members of the owners' families.

Boston, MUSEUM OF FINE ARTS: "Portrait of Lord Lyndhurst," "Lady Leicester and Her Son," "Portrait of Lady Lyndhurst," "Portrait of Charles James Fox," and others.

Brooklyn, MUSEUM: "Portrait of Miss Barnard."

Bryn Mawr, Pa., WISTER COLLECTION: "John Philip Kemble as Hamlet." "Portrait of John Philip Kemble."

Chicago, ART INSTITUTE: "Portrait of Mrs. Wolff."

Chicago, FISHER COLLECTION: "Portrait of James Banks West."

Cincinnati, MUSEUM ASSOCIATION: "Mrs. Francis Gregg and Master George Gregg."

Cincinnati, PRIVATE COLLECTIONS: Several examples.

Cleveland, MUSEUM OF ART: "Portrait of Benjamin West."

Cleveland, PRIVATE COLLECTIONS: Several examples.

Glen Cove, L. I., PRATT COLLECTION: "Portrait of Benjamin West."

Greenwich, Conn., SIMMONS COLLECTION: "Portrait of Louisa, Duchess of St. Albans."

Grosse Pointe, Mich., BOOTH COLLECTION: "Portrait of Lady Shaw."

Harrison, N. Y., AUGUSTE COLLECTION: "Portrait of Mrs. John W. Croker."

Hartford, WADSWORTH ATHENEUM: "Portrait of Benjamin West."

Huntington, L. I., MUSEUM: "Portrait of William Mills of Saxham Hall."

Indianapolis, TARKINGTON COLLECTION: "Portrait of George IV."

Lambton Castle, COUNTY DURHAM: "Portrait of Master Lambton."

London, NATIONAL GALLERY: "Portrait of Sir Philip Sansom," "Portrait of John Julius Angerstein," "Child with a Kid."

London, NATIONAL PORTRAIT GALLERY: "Portrait of Maria Calcott," "Portrait of Sir William Grant," "Portrait of Mrs. Siddons."

London, WALLACE COLLECTION: "Portrait of Miss Maria Siddons," "Portrait of the Countess of Blessington."

Manchester, Mass., COOLIDGE COLLECTION: "Portrait of Lady Maria Hamilton."

Montreal, ANGUS COLLECTION: "Portrait of Miss Harriet Day."

Moorestown, N. J., STOKES COLLECTION: "Portrait of Miss Storr."

Newport, REDWOOD LIBRARY AND ATHENAEUM: "Portrait of Abraham Redwood."

New York, FRICK COLLECTION: "Child with Flowers," "Portrait of Lady Julia Peel."

New York, METROPOLITAN MUSEUM OF ART: "Nature," "Portrait of Mrs. Wellesley," "Portrait of John Julius Angerstein," and others.

New York, PRIVATE COLLECTIONS AND SALES GALLERIES: Many examples.

Ottawa, NATIONAL GALLERY OF CANADA: "Portrait of Sir Alexander Mackenzie," "Portrait of Thomas Taylor, Esq."

Paris, LOUVRE: "Portrait of Lord Whitworth."

Philadelphia, HISTORICAL SOCIETY OF PENNSYLVANIA: "Portrait of Benjamin West."

Philadelphia, PENNSYLVANIA MUSEUM OF ART: "Portrait of Mrs. Fraser."

(*Continued*)

PLATE 64

LAWRENCE

1769-1830

Pinkie

United States National Gallery of Art, Washington

*

EARLY BRITISH SCHOOL

*

[*Continued from plate 63*] following year Lawrence was appointed painter to the king. At the age of twenty-four he was a full Academician. Lawrence, despite his substantial earnings, fell repeatedly into debt through his soft-hearted tolerance and support of his father's disastrous speculations. After the death in 1810 of a rival in popularity, Hoppner, Lawrence was enabled so to increase his fees as to achieve permanent financial security.

On the death of Benjamin West, Lawrence was made president of the Royal Academy. Through Lawrence's attempts to meet the growing demand for his portraits, the quality of his work somewhat deteriorated. He is, nevertheless, to be ranked as a distinguished member of the important eighteenth-nineteenth-century school of English portraiture.

Pinkie

By LAWRENCE

MARY MOULTON-BARRETT, who was born in 1783, died at the age of twelve. Her brother was that double-distilled family tyrant, Edward Barrett Moulton-Barrett, whose frail eldest daughter, Elizabeth, fifty years after little Pinkie's death, escaped to the freedom of a happy marriage by eloping with Robert Browning. Pinkie is, therefore, or would have been had she lived, the aunt of that distinguished poet, Elizabeth Barrett Browning.

From the picture in the United States National Gallery of Art, Washington

PRINCIPAL WORKS BY LAWRENCE

(Continued)

Pride's Crossing, Mass., FRICK COLLECTION: "Portrait of the Marquise du Blaizel."

St. Louis, JOHNSON COLLECTION: "Portrait of Georgiana, Duchess of Bedford."

San Marino, HUNTINGTON COLLECTION: "Portrait of the Duke of Wellington," "Miss Emily Anderson as Little Red Riding Hood," and others.

Washington, SMITHSONIAN INSTITUTION NATIONAL COLLECTION OF FINE ARTS: "Self-Portrait," "Lady Essex as Juliet," and others.

Washington, UNITED STATES NATIONAL GALLERY OF ART: "Lady Templeton and Her Child," "Pinkie."

Worcester, ART MUSEUM: "Portrait of the Hon. Miss Stuart."

PLATE 65

TURNER

1775-1851

The Fighting Téméraire

National Gallery, London

*

EARLY BRITISH SCHOOL

*

J. M. W. TURNER'S father was a London barber with a warm heart and uncommonly good horse sense. His son was an infant prodigy. At the age of seven the boy's drawings took their place as marketable objects beside his father's excellent wigs. Instead of putting the boy up in curls and satin pants, and waiting for the inevitable day when genius might flower, Turner's father decided to give him a sound education.

Even as pupils go, Turner was a particularly wretched one. While his masters droned on, Turner filled the margins of his textbooks with fragments of landscapes, with birds, and trees, and just designs. He had a number of drawing instructors at this time—Turner couldn't have chosen a better father for himself—one of whom deserves special attention. To him must go the credit for one of Art's most imperfect judgments. Exasperated and disgusted, this instructor, one Walton, took the young Turner by the hand and led him home to his father. And as he washed his hands of this unpleasant pupil, he thus addressed the barber: "Mr. Turner, it is no use; the boy will never do anything. He is impenetrably dull, sir! It is throwing your money away. Better make him a tinker, Sir, or a cobbler, than an artist." The poor father was heartbroken, but his faith was renewed when Turner, at the age of fifteen, received [Continued on plate 66]

The Fighting Téméraire

By TURNER

TURNER was out upon the Thames one day in 1838. It happened by chance that in late afternoon there came into view the old *Téméraire,* veteran of Trafalgar, being drawn by a tug to her ultimate destruction. One of Turner's companions turned to him and remarked, "Excellent subject for a picture." The painter made no comment, but a year later the picture appeared at the Royal Academy.

Turner's strikingly modern use of color is particularly advantageous in this canvas, for the golden glow that suffuses the atmosphere endows the old ship with the quality of ghostliness, a suggestion that perhaps the old hulk in some way sensed that this was to be her last voyage and that soon she was to join the company of vessels who had served men well but whose names were to be only memories and records in old registers.

From the picture in the National Gallery, London
—by permission

PLATE 66

TURNER

1775-1851

Crossing the Brook

National Gallery, London

———

*

EARLY BRITISH SCHOOL

*

[*Continued from plate 65*] a permanent position turning out architectural drawings. His benevolent employer thought his talent deserved finer opportunities and made it possible for him to enter the Royal Academy as a student.

His financial position improved and when in 1802 he was elected to the Royal Academy he had, at a remarkably tender age, achieved the distinction which other painters set as the goal of an entire life's activity.

Fame and wealth and (at times) unwarranted adulation left him cold. It was almost impossible to get him to sell a painting. He once remarked, after selling a picture, "I've lost one of my children this week." His comfortable and substantial income was derived chiefly from the sale of engraved reproductions. There were some who thought him a miser. His will, in which he bequeathed the major part of his fortune to his less fortunate comrades in art, is a tribute to his quiet, unobtrusive generosity.

In 1851 he suddenly disappeared from his customary haunts. Sensing, perhaps, that death was not far off, Turner had taken himself secretly to Chelsea, to a cottage by the river bank where he spent the time in seclusion. His close friends found him as he lay dying. Late in 1851 he passed away—still by the river and the ships.

Crossing the Brook

By TURNER

A LANDSCAPE painter may set down his easel before a scene and paint it as he sees it, without rearranging Nature. Or, in another fashion, he may freely alter what he sees, regrouping objects and things to suit the demands of a design which seems to him superior to Nature's.

Turner, like his great French predecessor, Claude Lorrain, took liberties with the things he saw. Here is a view made up of possibly more than ten separate scenes reassembled in an invented composition: the Tamar river, the headlands of Plymouth Sound, and bits here and there taken from the sketchbooks which are a record of Turner's wanderings. This has been the practice of all meritorious landscape painters.

From the picture in the National Gallery, London
—by permission

Boston, MUSEUM OF FINE ARTS: "The Slave Ship," "The Falls of the Rhine at Schaffhausen," "Rouen," and others including many loaned works.

Bryn Mawr, Pa., RADFORD COLLECTION: "On the Medway."

Cambridge, England, FITZWILLIAM MUSEUM: "Venice," "Sunset."

Cambridge, Mass., FOGG ART MUSEUM: "A Waterfall," "View of a Ruined Castle," "Mountainous Landscape."

Chicago, ART INSTITUTE: "Dutch Fishing Boats."

Cincinnati, HANNA COLLECTION: "Coblentz."

Cincinnati, TAFT COLLECTION INSTITUTE OF FINE ARTS: "Jedburgh Abbey," "The Lake of Brienz, Riggenberg Castle," "Folkestone," and others.

Cleveland, MUSEUM OF ART: "Carthage," "Queen Mab's Grotto."

Kansas City, NELSON GALLERY: "Fish Market on the Sands, Hastings."

London, NATIONAL GALLERY: "Crossing the Brook," "Calais Pier," "Edinburgh from Calton Hill," "The Fighting *Téméraire*," "Dido Building Carthage," "Frosty Morning," "Sun Rising through Vapor."

London, TATE GALLERY: "The Evening Star," "Norham Castle," "Hastings."

London, WALLACE COLLECTION: "Scarborough Castle," "Rainbow."

London, VICTORIA AND ALBERT MUSEUM: "Bridge over the Usk," "View of Richmond."

Manchester, Mass., COOLIDGE COLLECTION: "Landscape."

Montreal, REFORD COLLECTION: "Venice," "Plymouth."

Ottawa, NATIONAL GALLERY OF CANADA: "The Shipwreck."

New York, FRICK COLLECTION: "Cologne, Arrival of the Packet Boat, Evening," "Mortlake Terrace, Early Summer Morning," "Antwerp, Van Goyen Looking for a Subject," and others.

New York, METROPOLITAN MUSEUM OF ART: "The Whale Ship," "Grand Canal, Venice," "Norham Castle."

New York, PRIVATE COLLECTIONS AND SALES GALLERIES: Many examples.

New York, PUBLIC LIBRARY: "Staffa," "Fingal's Cave."

Philadelphia, WIDENER COLLECTION: "Keelmen Heaving in Coals by Moonlight," "Venice, Dogana and San Giorgio Maggiore."

San Marino, HUNTINGTON COLLECTION: "The Marriage of the Adriatic."

Toledo, MUSEUM OF ART: "Venice—the Campo Santo."

Washington, CORCORAN GALLERY: "Boats Carrying Out Anchors to the Dutch Men of War."

Washington, SMITHSONIAN INSTITUTION NATIONAL COLLECTION OF FINE ARTS: "Edinburgh, Painting of Sunlight and Air."

Washington, UNITED STATES NATIONAL GALLERY OF ART: "Mortlake Terrace," "Venetian Scene," "Van Tromp's Shallop at the Entrance of the Scheldt."

PLATE 67

CONSTABLE

1776-1837

The Hay Wain

National Gallery, London

*

EARLY BRITISH SCHOOL

*

JOHN CONSTABLE was born at East Bergholt, a little village fourteen miles from Sudbury, the birthplace of Gainsborough. He was the son of a well-to-do miller whose ambition it was to send his sons into one of the more prosaic professions, preferably the ministry. At seventeen, having shown little interest in scholarship, no proficiency in anything but penmanship, and no great interest in anything except the drawing of pictures, he left school; and from now on he devoted every moment of the time that could be spared from his duties about the mill to sketching the lanes and meadows of the countryside around his home. At this occupation he had the companionship of a friend, John Dunthorne, a plumber and glazier by trade. After a year of service in his father's mill, the older Constable so far relented in his opposition to his son's ambition as to permit him a visit to London that he might submit his sketches to those qualified to give an authoritative opinion upon the young man's prospects as an artist. Joseph Farrington, a landscape painter, was struck by his ability.

Much, however, as the young Constable had been encouraged to pursue his art, we find him writing in 1797, "I must now attend to my father's [*Continued on plate 68*]

The Hay Wain

By CONSTABLE

ON THE occasion of a visit to the Royal Academy in 1803, Constable wrote to an old friend, "There is almost nothing at the Exhibit worth stopping to look at. There is room for a painter of nature."

Constable had been a reverent student of the work of the Dutch painter, Ruysdael. This helped to form his style and strengthened his determination to devote his powers to portraying the neglected English landscape which he knew and loved so well.

The scene of "The Hay Wain" is near Flatford on the River Stour. The picture was sold to a Frenchman who exhibited it, together with two other Constables, at the Paris Salon. "The Hay Wain" was awarded a gold medal, and the entire Constable display elicited the unstinted praise of French artists. Constable's influence upon French landscape painting flowered and went to seed in the work of the Barbizon school.

From the picture in the National Gallery, London
—by permission

PLATE 68

CONSTABLE

1776-1837

The Cornfield

National Gallery, London

*

EARLY BRITISH SCHOOL

*

[*Continued from plate 67*] business. I see plainly that it must be my lot to walk through life in a path contrary to that which my inclination would lead me." Yet, two years after the date of this mood of discouragement, Constable resumed his pencil, never again to lay it aside. The recognition by artists which subsequently was accorded the young painter was withheld by the public. Although he was all but driven to take up the painting of portraits for a livelihood, he continued to devote himself above all else to the painting of the simple country landscape of his own loved Suffolk.

After a long and discouraging courtship conducted against parental opposition, he married; and when, subsequently, both he and his wife fell heir to substantial separate legacies, he was free to paint what he might please. In 1837, Constable, being then sixty-one years of age, was at work upon a picture of "Arundel Mill and Castle." He went out in the evening on some charitable business connected with the Artists' Benevolent Fund. Returning, he ate a hearty supper and went to bed. That midnight he died.

The Cornfield

By CONSTABLE

IN A LECTURE on the history of landscape painting, Constable delivered this rebuke to the wiseacres of art by which we may all profit. "The education," said he, "of a professed connoisseur being chiefly formed in the picture gallery and auction room, seldom enables him to perceive the vast difference between the mannerist and the genuine painter. To do this requires long and close study, and a constant comparison of the art with nature. So few among the buyers and sellers of pictures possess any knowledge so derived, that the works of the mannerists often bear as large a price in the market as those of the genuine painters. The difference is not understood by picture dealers, and thus, in a mercantile way, has a kind of art been propagated and supported from age to age, deserving only to be classed with the showy and expensive articles of drawing-room furniture."

From the picture in the National Gallery, London
—by permission

PRINCIPAL WORKS BY CONSTABLE

Boston, MUSEUM OF FINE ARTS: "Hampstead Heath," "Dedham Lock," "Landscape," "Self-Portrait," "Borrowdale," "His Native Village."

Chicago, ART INSTITUTE: "Stoke-by-Nayland, Suffolk."

Cincinnati, INSTITUTE OF THE FINE ARTS TAFT MUSEUM: "Dedham Mill."

Cincinnati, PRIVATE COLLECTIONS: Some examples.

Cleveland, MUSEUM OF ART: "Hampstead Heath."

Detroit, INSTITUTE OF FINE ARTS: "View of Norwich."

Hartford, WADSWORTH ATHENEUM: "Ripe Cornfield."

Lexington, Ky., WIDENER COLLECTION: "Flatford Mill."

London, NATIONAL GALLERY: "Flatford Mill," "The Cornfield," "The Hay Wain."

London, TATE GALLERY: "A Cornfield with Figures."

London, VICTORIA AND ALBERT MUSEUM: "Salisbury Cathedral," "Dedham Mill," "The Hay Wain."

Manchester, Mass., COOLIDGE COLLECTION: "The Hay Wain."

Montreal, PRIVATE COLLECTIONS: Several examples.

New York, FRICK COLLECTION: "Salisbury Cathedral."

New York, METROPOLITAN MUSEUM OF ART: "A Scene on the River Stour," "Tottenham Church."

New York, PRIVATE COLLECTIONS AND SALES GALLERIES: Many examples.

Ottawa, NATIONAL GALLERY OF CANADA: "Hampstead Heath."

Philadelphia, MUSEUM OF ART: "Dell in Helmingham Park."

Philadelphia, WIDENER COLLECTION: "Wivenhoe Park, Essex," "The White Horse."

Princeton, UNIVERSITY MUSEUM: Sketches of two landscapes.

Washington, PHILLIPS MEMORIAL GALLERY: "On the River Stour."

Washington, PRIVATE COLLECTIONS: Several examples.

Washington, SMITHSONIAN INSTITUTION NATIONAL COLLECTION OF FINE ARTS: "Dedham Vale — Summer Morning."

Washington, UNITED STATES NATIONAL GALLERY OF ART: "Salisbury Cathedral."

White Plains, N. Y., MILLER COLLECTION: "Dedham Lock."

Worcester, ART MUSEUM: "Mrs. Sophia Lloyd and Child."

PLATE 69

COX

1783-1859

The Skirt of the Forest

City Museum and Art Gallery, Birmingham

*

EARLY BRITISH SCHOOL

*

A BROKEN LEG took David Cox from the forge to the arts. His father, the black-smith of Deritend, near Birmingham, stopped Cox's schooling early to submit his son to the more practical learning of the blacksmith's art. A serious accident soon befell the boy, and the tedium of convalescence drove him to playing with a paint box. He loved it. But a blacksmith's son needs more than love. So Cox, after a short apprenticeship with a dealer in fancy goods, moved closer to his chosen career by becoming a scene-painter in a Birmingham theater. A visiting designer, impressed by his talents, had him promoted to the position of chief designer. In this capacity Cox spent five years before venturing a trip to London. There he befriended one John Varley, a water-color painter, from whom he learned much of his art. In 1805 he was painting landscapes in North Wales. These were exhibited in London and found favor with Colonel Windon, [*Continued on plate 70*]

The Skirt of the Forest

By COX

WE HAVE, in another instance, spoken of Freud in connection with Art. It is a notion of psychoanalysis, one, that the images and impressions of childhood live on into maturity, and, two, that an artist, even in a most deliberately objective work, presents material that is biographical and personal. This is what is meant by the "theory of persistence."

Place our two reproductions of Cox's landscapes before an efficient psychologist to test his hypothesis. What would he tell us?

He would probably say that Cox once had some intimate contact with horses, probably in childhood. And he would suggest further some incident in youth forceful enough to make the image of horses persist through his later years. So far, so good. Cox's father *was* a blacksmith; he worked at the forge. And it was there that he broke his leg. And came eventually to paint!

From the picture in the City Museum and Art Gallery, Birmingham
—by permission

PLATE 70

COX

1783-1859

Harlech Castle

Ashmolean Museum, Oxford

*

EARLY BRITISH SCHOOL

*

[*Continued from plate 69*] later to be Earl of Plymouth. A stroke of good fortune had thus freed him temporarily of the commercialism of theater painting.

After marrying his landlady's daughter in 1808, Cox took a cottage at Dulwich, where he produced hundreds of drawings for sale to art teachers—a very precarious livelihood. In 1813 he was elected to the Old Water-color Society and soon after was appointed drawing master of the Military College at Farnham. He lost this position quickly but managed to secure another much less lucrative position. For thirteen years he worked in dire poverty.

Then the tide turned suddenly. From 1835 to 1840 his output was enormous and sold well. He amassed wealth and acquired a home of his own near Birmingham where he died in 1859. It is difficult to say whether David Cox loved or regretted his profession. His last words were, "Good-bye, pictures." And we do not know to this day whether his sigh was one of regret or relief.

Harlech Castle

By COX

DAVID COX was a contemporary of John Constable (Plates 67 and 68). Whether he knew Constable's work, and if he did, whether he admired it, we do not definitely know. Judging from the contents of his pictures we are on solid ground if we assume that he both knew and admired. And perhaps tried to copy. And, if he did, failed.

Here is one good opportunity presented by this book to compare notes thoroughly and to understand why critics praise one artist and neglect another. We have two landscapes by Constable and two by Cox. We will assume that these groups of two are neither the best nor the worst of their works. We'll call them average.

Examine them closely without being technical. Don't look for design, or color, or treatment, or surface. Just look and let yourself react.

The chances are you'll favor the verdict of professional critics. There will be nothing to be ashamed of if you don't.

From the picture in the Ashmolean Museum, Oxford
—by permission

PRINCIPAL WORKS BY COX

Birmingham, CITY ART GALLERY: "The Skirt of the Forest."

London, BRITISH MUSEUM: Several examples.

London, VICTORIA AND ALBERT MUSEUM: "The Challenge."

Manchester, CITY ART GALLERY: Several examples.

Oxford, ASHMOLEAN MUSEUM: "Harlech Castle."

Washington, PHILLIPS MEMORIAL GALLERY: "Storm in the Vale of Clwyd."

Washington, SMITHSONIAN INSTITUTION NATIONAL COLLECTION OF FINE ARTS: "Landscape: Outskirts of a Wood."

West Manchester, Mass., CLARA WINTHROP COLLECTION: "Landscape."

PLATE 71

PETER DE WINT

1784-1849

A Cornfield

Victoria and Albert Museum, London

*

EARLY BRITISH SCHOOL

*

PETER DE WINT, descendant of a family of Dutch merchants once settled in America, was born in Staffordshire, in 1784. His father, a doctor, had established himself in England only a few years before. At the age of eighteen, De Wint began his studies in London with John Raffael Smith, a mezzotint engraver of considerable reputation. He soon developed an interest in landscape painting to which, in water-color and oils, he devoted his entire artistic career. He was poor, and earned a precarious livelihood instructing amateurs in the art of drawing. His painting stands outside the English tradition, uninfluenced by the art of his time, and in turn having little effect upon it.

A Cornfield

By PETER DE WINT

PETER DE WINT, whose ancestors came originally from Holland, painted atavistically. Though he was born in England and lived out his life in England, his works stemmed from the Dutch schools. Surface, meticulous and highly finished; composition, set on a low level, suggesting the flatlands of Holland; tonality, suffused and mellow, like Vermeer's.

"Cornfield"—the hour of rest in the farming day—is a subject first represented in painting by one of de Wint's "artistic grandparents," Pieter Breughel, the robust Dutch painter of the sixteenth century. And as "Cornfield" looks back for artistic precedents to the Holland of old, so does it predict, in feeling, our own American Inness.

From the picture in the Victoria and Albert Museum, London
—by permission

21

PRINCIPAL WORKS BY DE WINT

Birmingham, CITY ART GALLERY: "Church of Bray on Thames," "Courtyard of a Farm."

London, SOUTH KENSINGTON MUSEUM: "Lincoln Cathedral," "Wilsford, Lincolnshire."

Cambridge, SACHS COLLECTION: "Landscape" (drawing).

London, VICTORIA AND ALBERT MUSEUM: "In the Fen Country," "Wooded Landscape," "A Cornfield."

PLATE 72

LANDSEER

1802-1873

Shoeing the Bay Mare

Tate Gallery, London

*

LATER BRITISH SCHOOL

*

Sir Edwin Henry Landseer, one of the most popular painters of his century, was born in London in 1802. At the age of eight he was a proficient draftsman and, under the tutelage of his father, the painter John Landseer, developed so rapidly that the Academy exhibited in 1815 two pictures described in the catalogue as the work of "Master E. Landseer, 33 Foley Street." They were studies of a mule and of a dog. Landseer began his career with animal pictures and having once succeeded with them rarely, if ever, ventured into more imaginative fields.

Having once chosen his *métier*, Landseer was thorough about it. He studied carefully the rendering of animals in classical and modern art, and dissected every carcass he could get his hands on. "The Cat's Paw," which he exhibited at the age of twenty-two, had a sensational success. With the excellent price it brought, Landseer purchased a new home in which he lived until his death. Though he changed his style frequently and in later years succumbed to outright sentimentality, his popularity remained constant and undiminished. He was knighted in 1850, and in 1865 refused the presidency of the Academy. At the height of their popularity his paintings were fetching prices as high as $30,000. Landseer died in London in 1873, the most successful painter of his time.

Shoeing the Bay Mare

By LANDSEER

PAUL POTTER, a Dutchman, painted animals objectively— just animals. Morland used them to moralize. Audubon painted a beautiful catalogue of American birds for the sake of knowledge. Chirico, a modern, drew upon animal forms to enhance his fantastic designs. Pascin had an obsession about cats; he drew them because they had some strangely intimate connection with his life.

There are one thousand and one approaches to animal painting. Landseer's was the sentimental. He gave to animals the attributes of humans and placed them in situations comparable to those of every-day life. His dogs and horses laugh and cry; they are surprised or hurt, or tender or angry—never just creatures beautifully formed or stately in movement. He poses them for anecdote, not design. A wistful eye is more important in his work than a well-shaped muscle.

One Jacob Bell, who commissioned this portrait of his bay mare, "Old Betty," was wise to choose Landseer. For when, in the name of art, *portraits* are made of animals, certainly the sentimental painter will do them best. And to those who keep pets in their homes, and think of them as personalities, and bury them with honors, the art of Landseer will always be food for sentiment.

From the picture in the Tate Gallery, London
—by permission

PRINCIPAL WORKS BY LANDSEER

Bryn Mawr, Pa., RADFORD COLLECTION: "Portrait of a Lady."

London, NATIONAL GALLERY: "Spaniels of King Charles's Breed," "Dignity and Impudence."

London, TATE GALLERY: "Shoeing the Bay Mare," "The Hunted Stag," "Low Life – High Life."

Minneapolis, WALKER PUBLIC ART GALLERY: "Portrait of a Lady."

New York, METROPOLITAN MUSEUM OF ART: "Trophies of the Chase."

New York, PRIVATE COLLECTIONS: Several examples.

New York, PUBLIC LIBRARY: "A Landscape," "Sunset," "Dog in a Stable."

Washington, WALKER COLLECTION: "The Duke of Devonshire and Lady Louisa Egerton."

PLATE 73

MACLISE

1806-1870

The Death of Nelson

Westminster Palace, London

*

LATER BRITISH SCHOOL

*

DANIEL MACLISE was born at Cork, Ireland, where his father was stationed as a soldier in the Scots Highland regiment of the Cork Garrison. He attended the Cork School of Art and then served two years as clerk in a local bank. A fortunate accident launched his career in art. Sir Walter Scott was touring Ireland. Maclise happened to see him in a bookshop and sketched him as he browsed. The published lithographs of this chance portrait were immediate "best sellers." With the funds acquired through numerous commissions, Maclise was enabled to settle in London. There again, a portrait of the actor Kean, sketched as informally as Scott's, was a financial and popular success.

In 1829 Maclise enrolled in the Royal Academy Schools, won all of the important students' prizes, and within a year exhibited his first painting. His book illustrations for the novels of Dickens and "The Story of the Norman Conquest" were even better known than his historical paintings. Under the pseudonym of "Alfred Croquis" he drew a series of portraits for *Fraser's Magazine* which are an invaluable record of the artistic and literary life of his times. He refused both a knighthood and the presidency of the Academy, feeling, perhaps, that it was honor enough to have reproductions of his works in almost all of England's homes.

The Death of Nelson

By MACLISE

AN HOUR and ten minutes elapsed from the time when Nelson received his wound before Hardy could come to him. . . . "Well, Hardy," said Nelson, "how goes the day with us?" "Very well," replied Hardy; "ten ships have struck." . . . "I hope," said Nelson, "That none of our ships have struck!" Hardy answered, "There was no fear of that." Then, and not till then, Nelson spoke of himself: "I am going fast; it will be all over with me soon. Come nearer to me. Let my dear Lady Hamilton have my hair, and all other things belonging to me." . . . Hardy stood over him in silence for a moment or two, then knelt again and kissed his forehead. "Who is that?" said Nelson; and being informed, he replied, "God bless you, Hardy," and then Hardy left him—forever.— SOUTHEY, *Life of Nelson*.

From the picture in Westminster Palace, London
—by permission

PRINCIPAL WORKS BY MACLISE

Dublin, MUSEUM: "The Wedding of Richard of Clare to the Daughter of Dermont McMorragh, King of Leinster."

London, TATE GALLERY: "Charles Dickens," "Malvolio and the Countess."

London, PALACE OF WESTMINSTER: "The Death of Nelson," "The Meeting of Wellington and Blücher."

There are no well-known works by Maclise in public galleries in the United States.

PLATE 74

WATTS

1817-1904

Hope

Tate Gallery, London

*

LATER BRITISH SCHOOL

*

GEORGE FREDERICK WATTS was born in London in 1817. His family had come originally from Wales. After a period of study at the Royal Academy and with William Behnes, a sculptor, he first presented a picture publicly in 1837. Not long afterwards, he was given a scholarship which permitted him to spend four years in Italy. On this trip he turned out an enormous number of portraits. Soon after his return to England he received a substantial prize in a competition for decorations to be placed in the House of Parliament. Prompted by a lively interest in Greek sculpture, he accompanied an archeological expedition which set out to discover the original site of Halicarnassus. Thereafter, no event of special significance enlivens an account of his life. Setting up few confining limits and finding inspiration in almost any subject that momentarily caught his fancy, Watts was a prolific artist and produced much more than most of his contemporaries.

Hope

By WATTS

G EORGE FREDERICK WATTS believed that the first objective of painting was moral improvement. He wished that his work might lead to better ideas and nobler conceptions. William Hazlitt many years before had made a general statement about morality in painting which is one possible criticism of this work: "Indifferent pictures, like dull people, must absolutely be moral."

Watts frequently tried to symbolize a human emotion or feeling by the use of a figure arbitrarily posed and clothed—one which did not necessarily follow the formula or iconography of traditional Western painting.

"Hope" is undoubtedly the most popular of all Watts' works. It is simple, pure allegory, and successfully conveys some of the meaning which we ordinarily associate with the word. It is not being facetious to remark that this picture has probably appeared more often than any other on illustrated calendars. This fact should be considered a tribute to the achievement of Watts' specific aim in painting it, for if one stands before a formal listing of days that are to come and has certain wishes to be fulfilled, certainly the juxtaposition of "Hope" is an effective and heart-warming proximity.

From the picture in the Tate Gallery, London
—by permission

74

PRINCIPAL WORKS BY WATTS

London, National Portrait Gallery: "Thomas Carlyle," "Earl Russell," "Cardinal Manning."

London, Tate Gallery: "Love and Life," "Hope," "Life's Illusions."

New York, Metropolitan Museum of Art: "Ariadne in Naxos."

Washington, Smithsonian Institution National Collection of Fine Arts: "Love and Life."

PLATE 75

BROWN

1821-1893

The Last of England

Tate Gallery, London

*

LATER BRITISH SCHOOL

*

FORD MADOX BROWN was born of English parents at Calais in 1821. His first artistic training he received in Belgium under the tutelage of Van Hauselaer and Baron Wappers. The Belgian school in Brown's time excelled in documentary painting and taught its followers to stage scenes dramatically, to embellish them with authentic detail, in short, to be "stage managers" of their pictures. This lesson Brown learned well.

He returned to London in 1846 to launch a career distinguished by an enormous output of historical pictures and a close association with the Pre-Raphaelite Brotherhood, to which he was attracted by a warm sympathy with its ideals. Dante Gabriel Rossetti (Plate 76) was one of his pupils.

Between 1850 and 1877 Brown, a very slow painter, completed most of his historical pictures. Unlike most artists of his generation whose commercial activity extended only to illustrating books, Brown became an active member of a prominent firm of decorators and in this capacity executed the designs for stained-glass windows and wall decorations for many of England's great public buildings.

Brown died in London in 1893, survived by his second wife and a daughter who married into the Rossetti family.

The Last of England

By BROWN

DURING the nineteenth century thousands migrated from England to the four corners of the earth. Brown had a friend named Thomas Woolner, a sculptor, who was about to sail to Australia. Brown came aboard his ship to bid him good-bye. There he watched the emigrants and observed, as he says, the indifferent attitude of the lower classes towards the ending of old loyalties contrasted with the evident regrets of the middle classes. To what and to whom the lower classes owed allegiance, save themselves and the hope of becoming middle classes in some other land, we cannot imagine. Brown chose the fearful folk, forlorn of hope, to be his subjects.

"Without heeding the art of any other people or country," he wrote, "I have tried to render the scene as it would seem. I thought it necessary to imitate the minuteness of detail which would be visible in the same conditions of full daylight in order to accentuate the intimate emotion of the subject." This statement comes most appropriately from the pen of a Pre-Raphaelite. It epitomizes their aspirations in art.

"The Last of England." The last of England, indeed!—when a man of art, who should be first a man of life, finds in *his* class alone the praiseworthy virtues.

From the picture in the Tate Gallery, London
—by permission

PRINCIPAL WORKS BY BROWN

London, NATIONAL GALLERY: "Christ Washing Peter's Feet."

Manchester, CITY ART GALLERY: "Work."

Wilmington, Del., ROCKFORD: "Romeo and Juliet."

London, TATE GALLERY: "Lear and Cordelia," "The Last of England."

Roseland, N. J., MICHAEL STILLMAN COLLECTION: "Portrait of Mrs. William James Stillman."

PLATE 76

ROSSETTI

1828-1882

Monna Pomona

Tate Gallery, London

*

LATER BRITISH SCHOOL

*

DANTE GABRIEL ROSSETTI was born in London in 1828; he was of Italian descent. He studied first in the schools of the Royal Academy and later with Madox Brown.

Rossetti was a poet too; he adored Dante and could recite his entire works from memory. Since he sensed, quite accurately, that his art would not be warmly accepted by his fellow Englishmen, he admitted openly that it was created for the benefit and appreciation of his immediate friends and sympathizers who shared with him the aims and aspirations of the Pre-Raphaelite movement.

At the age of twenty-two he met one Eleanor Siddal, a modiste, whom he later married. It is the image of her and of her peculiar wistful moods which frequents so much of his painting. Rossetti was not without affectation. Perhaps the most extreme gesture of his life was the placing of a volume of poems in manuscript in his wife's grave after her sudden death in 1863. He had the good sense to exhume them some years later; this added aura has increased their popularity among highly sentimental people.

Rossetti died in 1882. Death for him was the only successful escape from the sordidness and banality of life in early Victorian England to which he was not able properly to adjust either himself or his art.

Monna Pomona

By ROSSETTI

IT CAN be said fairly of the Pre-Raphaelite movement that the road to it was paved with good intentions. Rossetti was more deliberately mystical than Millais or Hunt, who founded the movement with him. His paintings are less simple and more pretentious.

To one who might, by chance, catch sight of this picture without knowing either its title or purpose, there might certainly be much to be puzzled about. For one thing, this person is surely a woman, but there are portions of her that seem better fitted to the body of a man. In her right hand she holds an apple insecurely. Her left hand either fondles a necklace or, conceivably, makes a weak attempt at strangulation. What does this subject mean? It doesn't matter. All that matters is that our grandparents liked this picture and found in it something that permitted them to run off spiritually to a world which must have seemed nobler and more respectful of worthy aspirations and pure emotions.

From the picture in the Tate Gallery, London
—by permission

PRINCIPAL WORKS BY ROSSETTI

Boston, GARDNER COLLECTION: "Love's Litany."

Boston, MUSEUM OF FINE ARTS: "Before the Battle."

Boston, SEARS COLLECTION: "Tristan et la Belle Iseult."

Chicago, ART INSTITUTE: "Beata Beatrix."

Detroit, INSTITUTE OF ARTS: "The Fight for a Woman."

London, NATIONAL GALLERY: "Ecce Ancilla Domini" (The Annunciation).

London, TATE GALLERY: "Beata Beatrix," "The Passover in the Holy Family," "Monna Pomona."

New York, METROPOLITAN MUSEUM OF ART: "Lady Lilith."

New York, PETERS COLLECTION: "Joan of Arc."

Wilmington, Del., BANCROFT ESTATE: "Veronica Veronese," "Lady Lilith," "Mnemosyne or the Lamp of Memory," "La Bella Mano," "Water Willow," and studies.

PLATE 77

MILLAIS

1829-1896

The Blind Girl

City Museum and Art Gallery, Birmingham

*

LATER BRITISH SCHOOL

*

JOHN EVERETT MILLAIS, descendant of a family long established on the Isle of Jersey, was born at Southampton in 1829. The earliest years of his life were spent in Brittany where, as a child, he devoted most of his time to sketching. When his family moved to London in 1838 Sir Martin Shee, president of the Royal Academy, was so deeply impressed by his youthful ability that he permitted Millais to be enrolled in the Academy School at the unprecedented age of eleven. When he was first led into the "antique room" of the school, his fellow pupils, some four times his age, were so astonished they first believed it was a joke. But soon they saw that the boy was an infant prodigy. At seventeen, an age when most youths were still scribbling Latin and Greek, Millais exhibited his first paintings.

It was at his home that the idea of the Pre-Raphaelite Brotherhood was born. Hunt, Rossetti, Woolner (a sculptor) and Millais were examining reproductions of the frescoes at Campo Santo, Pisa, and the conversation that followed is believed to have produced the decision to organize the movement. Millais was its initial [Continued on plate 78]

The Blind Girl

By MILLAIS

THESE eyes, though clear
To outward view, of blemish or of spot,
Bereft of light, their seeing have forgot,
Nor to their idle orbs doth sight appear
Of sun, or moon, or star, throughout the year,
Of man, or woman. Yet I argue not
Against Heaven's hand or will, nor bate a jot
Of heart or hope; but still bear up and steer
Right onward.

—MILTON.

From the picture in the City Museum and Art Gallery, Birmingham
—by permission

PLATE 78

MILLAIS

1829-1896

The Boyhood of Raleigh

Tate Gallery, London

*

LATER BRITISH SCHOOL

*

[*Continued from plate 77*] "victim." His "Carpenter's Shop," a new version of an episode from the life of Christ, was the first Pre-Raphaelite picture to evoke the extreme animosity of critics. Charles Dickens, by what right we do not know, contributed this insult. "The picture is mean, odious, revolting, and repulsive"; a description as meaningless as it is bitter. So heated was the furor that Queen Victoria, ill and bedridden, commanded that the painting be brought to her for inspection.

Presumably it passed. For in the years that followed, public antipathy to the ideas of Pre-Raphaelitism gradually softened, and Millais, drifting from its center, came into popularity and wealth. Up to the year of his death, 1896, he was prolific in his art and diffuse in his choice of subject. There was enough of his painting and a variety of styles to please any taste. He was respected and applauded, and England took notice of his eminence by bestowing upon him a baronetcy, ample restitution for the abuse and derision that greeted his youthful works.

The Boyhood of Raleigh

By MILLAIS

"SIR WALTER RALEGH was descended from an antient Family in *Devonshire* which was seated in that County before the Conquest; and was fourth son of *Walter Ralegh* Esq; of *Fardel* in the Parish of *Cornwood,* eight miles East of *Plymouth,* by his third wife *Catharine,* Daughter of Sir *Philip Champernon* of *Modbury,* and relict of *Otho Gilbert,* of *Compton* in *Devon,* Esq; He was born in the Year 1552, at *Hayes,* a pleasant farm of his Father's in the Parish of *Budley,* in that part of *Devonshire* bordering Eastward upon the Sea, near where the *Ottery* discharges itself into the *British Channel.* After he had passed thro' his first Education at School, he was transplanted to the University of *Oxford.*"—THO. BIRCH, in preface to Raleigh's "Works."

Millais, *mirabile dictu,* has history to support his imagination. ". . . in that part of Devonshire bordering Eastward upon the Sea." Yes, there Raleigh could have sat, by the shore, and listened to old hands tell tales about the new lands beyond the horizon.

From the picture in the Tate Gallery, London
—by permission

PRINCIPAL WORKS BY MILLAIS

Birmingham, ART GALLERY: "The Blind Girl."

London, TATE GALLERY: "Christ in the House of His Parents," "The Boyhood of Raleigh."

Manchester, CITY ART GALLERY: "Autumn Leaves," "Portrait of Mrs. Charles Freeman."

New York, PATTERSON COLLECTION: "Head of a Girl."

New York, METROPOLITAN MUSEUM OF ART: "Ellen Terry as Portia."

Omaha, MARTIN COLLECTION: "Little Red Riding Hood."

Ottawa, NATIONAL GALLERY OF CANADA: "Portrait of the Marquess of Lorne."

Wilmington, Del., ROCKFORD: "The White Cockade."

PLATE 79

BURNE-JONES

1833-1898

King Cophetua and the Beggar Maid

Tate Gallery, London

*

LATER BRITISH SCHOOL

*

SIR EDWARD BURNE-JONES was born at Birmingham in 1833. At Oxford, where he was reading theology in preparation for the priesthood, he met Rossetti and William Morris, whose stimulating friendships turned his interest from religion to art.

Burne-Jones had no formal training in the arts and no instruction in the craft of painting until Rossetti, whom he later joined in London, taught him the A B C, of course, in the language of Rossetti. But the pupil, after extensive travels in Italy (some in the company of Ruskin), finally developed a personal style which more effectively employed the principles enunciated and practised by his master.

For many years his paintings, only part of his prodigious output, attracted no attention. Related arts engaged his interest. In collaboration with William [*Continued on plate 80*]

King Cophetua
and the Beggar Maid

By BURNE-JONES

HER ARMS across her breast she laid;
   She was more fair than words can say;
Barefooted came the beggar maid
   Before the king Cophetua.
In robe and crown the king stept down,
   To meet and greet her on her way;
"It is no wonder," said the lords,
   "She is more beautiful than day."

As shines the moon in clouded skies,
   She in her poor attire was seen;
One praised her ankles, one her eyes,
   One her dark hair and lovesome mien.
So sweet a face, such angel grace,
   In all the land had never been.
Cophetua sware a royal oath:
   "This beggar maid shall be my queen!"
                    —ALFRED, LORD TENNYSON

From the picture in the Tate Gallery, London
—by permission

PLATE 80

BURNE-JONES

1833-1898

The Star of Bethlehem

City Museum and Art Gallery, Birmingham

*

LATER BRITISH SCHOOL

*

[*Continued from plate 79*] Morris he designed stained-glass windows for Oxford and Salisbury Cathedrals and a series of mosaic decorations for the American Protestant Church in Rome.

Around 1870 Burne-Jones acquired enormous popularity. The aesthetes of England adored him with deep and profound reverence. "The Temple of Aesthetic," Grosvenor House, where his works were exhibited, was always jammed to the doors by a mob which blocked the view. Rossetti looked on, proud of his original discovery, happy in the success of his pupil. "The work of Burne-Jones," he pronounced, "is a unique work, not only in English art, but in the art of all times."

A centenary exhibition, held in 1933, revived interest in Burne-Jones' work without confirming the judgment of his spiritual father.

The Star of Bethlehem

By BURNE-JONES

NOW WHEN Jesus was born in Bethlehem of Judaea in the days of Herod the king, behold, there came wise men from the east to Jerusalem, saying, Where is he that was born King of the Jews? for we have seen his star in the east, and are come to worship him. Then Herod, when he had privily called the wise men, enquired of them diligently what time the star appeared. When they had heard the king, they departed; and, lo, the star, which they saw in the east, went before them, till it came and stood over where the young child was. When they saw the star, they rejoiced with exceeding great joy. And when they were come into the house, they saw the young child with Mary his mother, and fell down, and worshiped him: and when they had opened their treasures, they presented unto him gifts; gold, and frankincense, and myrrh.—MATTHEW II.

Here is the Bible as a Pre-Raphaelite conceived it. And here is the work of an artist who shows in his painting a love of the Italian primitives, an imagination colored by the Arthurian legends, and a wide experience in the designing of stained glass.

From the picture in the City Museum and Art Gallery, Birmingham
—by permission

PRINCIPAL WORKS BY BURNE-JONES

Birmingham, CORPORATION ART GALLERY: "The Star of Bethlehem."

Boston, MUSEUM OF FINE ARTS: "Le Chant d'Amour."

Chicago, ART INSTITUTE: "Cupid's Hunting Fields," and a number of drawings.

Liverpool, WALKER ART GALLERY: "Sponsa di Libano."

London, SOUTH KENSINGTON MUSEUM: "The Mill."

London, TATE GALLERY: "King Cophetua and the Beggar Maid."

Manchester, CITY ART GALLERY: "Sibylla Delphica."

Minneapolis, INSTITUTE OF ARTS: "Wedding of Psyche."

New York, WINTHROP COLLECTION: "Day," "Danaë Watching the Building of the Brazen Tower," "Pan and Psyche," "Flamma Vestalis," and several drawings and studies.

PLATE 81

YEAMES

1835-1918

"When did you last see your father?"

Walker Art Gallery, Liverpool

———

*

LATER BRITISH SCHOOL

*

THE FAMILY of William Frederick Yeames lived in South Russia, where his father, an official of the British Foreign Service, was serving as consul in the city of Taganrog. Here he was born. At an early age Yeames moved to Dresden, which was at that time an important pedagogical center of academic painting, to study as a pupil of Westmacott and later of George Scharf. At twenty-five he came to London and soon afterwards presented his first exhibited painting at the Royal Academy. He was made an associate of this organization in 1867 and rose to full membership eleven years later.

Yeames was not a versatile painter, limiting his work to pictures of historical interest. Of these he painted many; none has ever approached the public popularity of the canvas here reproduced. He held for many years the position—chiefly honorary—of librarian to the Academy and when finally he resigned he settled for the remainder of his life at Teignmouth, where he died in 1918.

"When did you last see your father?"

By YEAMES

WHEN the Puritan Revolution succeeded in England, no effort was spared to seek out and track down the old adherents to the cause of Royalism. So thorough was the hunt and so important its objectives that the Roundheads stopped at nothing to ferret out their enemies. It is contrary to all established notions of morality and chivalrous behavior for a child to betray his parent. It is assumed that there must be some force in biology that makes a kinship of the blood superior to the demands or opinions of any given moment. Yeames portrays a small and delicate child being quizzed by a group of somber and serious Roundheads who are hoping that innocence and naïveté will inadvertently disclose the whereabouts of his unfortunate parents. The boy's sister, even more sympathetically pictured, awaits her turn at the bar and, in the fashion of women, becomes slightly hysterical at the thought of the ordeal that is to come.

From the picture in the Walker Art Gallery, Liverpool
—by permission

PRINCIPAL WORKS BY YEAMES

Glasgow, CORPORATION ART GAL-
LERY: "Prisoners of War."

Liverpool, WALKER ART GALLERY:
"When did you last see your
father?"

London, TATE GALLERY: "Amy
Robsart."

There are no well-known works by
Yeames in public galleries in the
United States.

PLATE 82

ORCHARDSON

1831-1910

Napoleon on the Bellerophon

Tate Gallery, London

*

SCOTTISH SCHOOL

*

THERE IS NOT much to be said about the life of William Orchardson that differs greatly from a description of the careers of most popular painters of his generation. He was a Scotchman, a native of Edinburgh, and his training was received in the academies. He came to London when he was a little more than thirty and soon was accepted as an associate of the Royal Academy. In 1877 this institution granted him full membership.

Orchardson exhibited regularly at the Academy, producing from year to year a series of pictures which were popular with the English public and which brought him security and an established position in the British world of art.

Napoleon on the Bellerophon

By ORCHARDSON

WHEN THE end came for Napoleon at Waterloo and the prospect of any future campaign to re-establish his conquests seemed hopeless, he tried desperately to reach the coast of France, hoping to escape to the United States. The attempt failed and Napoleon was forced to surrender to the British ship *Bellerophon*.

This was a moment a man might say fittingly, "I wish to be alone." His faithful, worshipful generals respect a great man's need of solitude. They stand away, waiting for him to finish his thoughts, prepared, it would seem, to follow any decision.

Historical painting finds excellent material in solemn moments and has been more successful portraying defeat and desperation than the exultation of victory. Here, once the picture has fixed a point of narration, we may sit back at leisure and build around it the Napoleonic legend; the great achievements that preceded this isolated moment, and the lonely, bitter years that were to follow it.

Meissonier's "1814" (Plate 49) describes another episode of Napoleon's career without stimulating in us as much desire to fill in the beginning and the end of the story the painting tells.

From the picture in the Tate Gallery, London
—by permission

82

PRINCIPAL WORKS BY ORCHARDSON

Brooklyn, INSTITUTE: "The Queen of Swords."

Glasgow, CORPORATION ART GALLERY: "The Farmer's Daughter."

Edinburgh, NATIONAL GALLERY OF SCOTLAND: "Master Baby."

London, TATE GALLERY: "Her First Dance," "Napoleon on the *Bellerophon*."

PLATE 83

PETTIE

1839-1893

The Vigil

Tate Gallery, London

*

SCOTTISH SCHOOL

*

THE CAREER of John Pettie followed the normal, sedate design of the lives of most popular British painters of his century. He was born at Edinburgh in 1839. An early manifestation of talent in sketching brought him to the attention of James Drummond, a distinguished member of the Royal Scottish Academy. There at the age of sixteen Pettie began his studies, and three years later exhibited his first canvas. From Academy to Academy, Scotch to British; Pettie moved to London where, at twenty-one, he made his artistic debut. Success came quickly. In 1866 he was elected [*Continued on plate 84*]

The Vigil

By PETTIE

THE NINETEENTH century discovered the Middle Ages—emotionally and inaccurately. In literature and the arts, whether it be in Scott or the atavistic idealism of the Pre-Raphaelite Brotherhood, the medieval age was examined through rose-colored glasses. The artists of Victorian England, caring little for research and the science of history, abstracted from that period all of its imagined virtues and left untouched the record of its more abundant horrors.

They imagined, naïvely or willfully, that the inspiration of life in the Middle Ages stemmed only from noble sources; that Europe then was peopled by human beings perfect in the body and the spirit; that all men were big and strong and brave; that all women were virtuous and angelic; that life was spent in the search of justice; that love was everywhere.

Since then the scholars and pedants have got to work. And we know that popular art made poppycock of history. The truth, so hard to bear, tells us of palaces that stank, manners that were filthy, kings who were cripples, knights who were tubercular wrecks, and fair maidens who were deformed and dwarfs.

No reason to be angry. What if the nineteenth century did idealize and romanticize? Don't we remember how as children—like Miniver Cheevy—we sat dreaming in the shade of a tree, yearning for a world of nobility and chivalry? Painters too have wanted to run away from the world which sordidly surrounded them.

From the picture in the Tate Gallery, London
—by permission

PLATE 84

PETTIE

1839-1893

Two Strings to Her Bow

Corporation Art Gallery, Glasgow

*

SCOTTISH SCHOOL

*

[*Continued from plate 83*] to associate membership in the Royal Academy and in 1874 to the full membership made vacant by the death of Landseer. He died in Hastings in 1893.

Pettie's painting was literary. Inspired by the historical novels of his countryman, Sir Walter Scott, he turned to the Middle Ages for his subject matter. The British public of his time, cultivating identical interests, appreciated his painting and gave him a measure of popularity which afforded him a comfortable life and academic prestige.

Two Strings to Her Bow

By PETTIE

A SUIT of men's clothing preserved in the London Museum has precisely the same cut as the costume of these two dandies. And so we know, beyond the shadow of a doubt, that the year was 1810, in the reign of the lunatic George III—the age of the Regency and Beau Brummel, of high fashion, and daring courtship.

Of mam'selle's dilemma, Elizabeth Barrett Browning had this to say in rhyme:

> She has laughed as softly as if she sighed,
> She has counted six, and over,
> Of a purse well filled, and a heart well tried—
> Oh, each a worthy lover!
> They "give her time"; for her soul must slip
> Where the world has set the grooving;
> She will lie to none with her fair red lip:
> But love seeks truer loving.

From the picture in the Corporation Art Gallery, Glasgow
—by permission

PRINCIPAL WORKS BY PETTIE

Glasgow, CORPORATION ART GAL-
LERY: "Two Strings to Her Bow,"
"A Sword-and-Dagger Fight."

London, TATE GALLERY: "Self-
Portrait," "The Vigil."

Melbourne, ART GALLERY: "The
Arrest for Witchcraft."

Sheffield, ART GALLERY: "Treason," "The Drum-Head Court-
Martial."

There are no well-known works of Pettie in public galleries
in the United States.

PLATE 85

HOLIDAY

1839-1927

Dante and Beatrice

Walker Art Gallery, Liverpool

*

LATER BRITISH SCHOOL

*

HENRY HOLIDAY, born at London in 1839, attended the schools of the Royal Academy where he obtained the training which, developing a natural bent for monumental design, led to a successful career in mural decoration and the art of stained glass. He was strongly attracted to classical art and, unlike many of his contemporaries who based their praise on copies, made many visits to Athens to study first-hand the sculpture of ancient Greece. "Panathenaia," perhaps the most successful of his pseudo-classical pictures, was based upon his direct observation of the Parthenon frieze.

Holiday is best known for his obsessional preoccupation with, and devotion to, the life and works of Dante. This interest had been fully developed before he reached the age of nineteen and drove him, literally drove him, to unbelievable extremes in seeking perfect authenticity for his "Dante" pictures. Of these there are many, the most popular being the "Dante and Beatrice" here reproduced. Behind the painting of this canvas is a long and tedious history: a trip to Florence, a study of thirteenth-century Italian buildings, rummaging in archives, minute examination of street pavements, the making of clay models for the figures, etc., etc. Excessive research has too often been the death of art.

Dante and Beatrice

By HOLIDAY

THUS, Dante: "On my return I set myself to seek out that lady whom my master had named to me. . . . The matter was spoken of by many in terms scarcely courteous; through the which I had oftenwhiles many troublesome hours. And by this it appeared (to wit, by the false and evil rumor which seemed to misfame me of vice) that she who was the destroyer of all evil and the queen of all good, coming where I was, denied me her most sweet salutation, in the which alone was my blessedness. . . . And now I became possessed of such grief that, parting myself from all others, I went into a lonely place to bathe the ground with most bitter tears."

Thus, Holiday.

There are few of Holiday's works in public galleries, and none in the United States.

From the picture in the Walker Art Gallery, Liverpool
—by permission

PLATE 86

MOORE

1841-1893

A Summer Night

Walker Art Gallery, Liverpool

*

LATER BRITISH SCHOOL

*

THE MOORES WERE a family of artists. Albert Joseph Moore was one of three sons of William Moore, of York, portraitist and landscape painter. His two brothers, John and Henry, also followed the profession of their father.

Albert was instructed first by his meticulous, painstaking father, and later at the schools of the Royal Academy. This institution never invited Moore to join its membership, presumably for the reason that a number of his irreverent remarks had reached the ears of its more august directors. But the lack of this overrated conventional distinction proved no handicap. Commissions came to Moore in great numbers: decorations for country houses, churches and theaters. Almost always he drew from biblical history for his subject matter.

Moore, as, alas, his paintings show too well, was fastidious to the point of nausea. Refinement was his end and his beginning. When he died in 1893, Whistler is supposed to have said, "Albert Moore, poor fellow, the greatest artist England might have cared for and called her own." Under the burden of this sardonic epitaph, the remains of Albert Joseph Moore must rest uneasily and fretfully in their grave.

A Summer Night

By MOORE

WHEN Albert Moore was halfway through this panel Death began to stare him in the face. He was told suddenly that he must undergo an operation. The chance of recovery was poor. But he proceeded calmly to finish the picture before tempting Fate. Unruffled and resolute, he refined the minutest details, carefully measured out the garlands, put the final touches in their place.

With what we know now of psychology, it is safe to assume that an artist, sensing that he is about to die, will probably make his last work the image of his personal Paradise. "A Summer Night" has much to support this theory. Moore loved flowers; he could not paint unless they cluttered up his studio. Here they are in formal profusion. Exquisite details, lovely vases, old brocades delighted him. They too are present in his canvas. But now, what of these luscious maidens? What a field day for a Freudian!

From the picture in the Walker Art Gallery, Liverpool
—by permission

PRINCIPAL WORKS BY MOORE

Birmingham, CITY ART GALLERY:
"The Dreamers."

Liverpool, WALKER ART GALLERY:
"A Summer Night."

London, TATE GALLERY: "Blossoms."

There are no well-known works of Moore in public galleries in the United States.

PLATE 87

SOMERSCALES

1842-1928

Off Valparaiso

Tate Gallery, London

*

LATER BRITISH SCHOOL

*

THOMAS SOMERSCALES, son of a shipmaster, was a man of the sea, and living near it, on it, he knew it well and loved it. And therefore painted it.

At twenty-one he took a post as teacher in the Royal British Navy and spent seven years cruising the Pacific; thereafter he lived in coastal towns and on the ocean. As a banker turns to golf for relaxation, so Somerscales painted for amusement, not for exhibition or sale. Like the Douanier Rousseau, postman-painter of France, self-taught, an amateur, naïve, Somerscales made art an avocation.

His painting is of sailing ships, of his own direct experience, of a life he loved, of a career he knew well. His pictures, then, should not be judged by aesthetes; better, sailors. Somerscales' paintings are successful if an old salt, examining them, can recreate a part of his own experience, thinking, yes, this was the look of the sky and the feel of the sea; or, this is the way *we* set our sails; or, she was a ship well built and rode the water gracefully.

The criterion—here alone justified—is authenticity.

Off Valparaiso

By SOMERSCALES

"OFF VALPARAISO." Not anywhere, on any ocean, in any latitude. "Off Valparaiso": a seafaring man knows where it is and what it means. Latitude: 33°. Going north or going south, from the Horn or to the Horn, the temper of the sea changes here, off the Chilean coast.

In June, 1834, Richard Dana, two years before the mast, homeward bound, heading towards the Horn, thus described it:

"There began now to be a decided change in the appearance of things. The days became shorter and shorter, the sun running lower in its course each day, and giving less and less heat, and the nights so cold as to prevent our sleeping on deck; the Magellan Clouds in sight, of a clear, moonless night; the skies looking cold and angry; and, at times, a long, heavy, ugly sea, setting in from the southward, told us what we were coming to."

From the picture in the Tate Gallery, London
—by permission

PRINCIPAL WORKS BY SOMERSCALES

London, TATE GALLERY: "Off
Valparaiso."

Sheffield, ART GALLERY: "Before
the Gale," "Man Overboard."

There are no well-known works by Somerscales in public galleries
in the United States.

PLATE 88

PARSONS

1847-1920

Poplars in a Thames Valley

Art Gallery and Industrial Museum, Aberdeen

*

LATER BRITISH SCHOOL

*

ALFRED PARSONS was born at Beckington, Somerset, in 1847. After a private education he became a clerk in the General Post Office. Though he had no formal training in art, he resigned his clerkship two years after becoming a civil servant to devote his life to painting. Before his first picture was exhibited at the Royal Academy in 1871, he was engaged in illustrating books. In 1897 the Academy granted him an associate membership; he attained full membership in 1911. He visited Japan in 1892 and remained there for two years. The result of this trip was a book called "Notes on Japan," published four years after his return to England. The art of the Orient evidently made no impression upon his style. From 1914 to 1920, the year he died, Parsons was president of the Royal Society of Painters in Water Colour.

Poplars in a Thames Valley

By PARSONS

REBELS in art have made great sacrifices. Painting the world the way they saw it and in a style which best expressed their vision often brought a life of poverty and neglect, frequently of persecution. The original painters of the Impressionist School suffered to some degree this unfortunate fate. We cannot well imagine today, now that Impressionism and its methods are so much a part of the tools of painting, what terrible abuse their contemporaries hurled at them. Their pictures found few buyers. Hunger frequently stared them in the face.

In the world of art, time and habit are softeners. We take for granted today what was cheaply ridiculed only a decade ago. They hissed Stravinsky in the years before the War. Today he is invited to lecture at America's foremost university. And so it was with Impressionism. The more people saw of it, the more acceptable it became. Their eyes, accustomed to the new technique by habit and repetition, began to take for granted this way of looking at nature.

It is always the followers in painting who reap the fruit of innovation. When Impressionism became "safe," that is, when people began to accept it, conventional painters ventured the new technique. Alfred Parsons, academician, was one of these. "Poplars in a Thames Valley" is what we may call an impressionistic painting. It would pass any academic jury. No furor, no fuss. It is easy to travel a path cleared by pioneers.

From the picture in the Art Gallery and Industrial Museum, Aberdeen
—by permission

PRINCIPAL WORKS BY PARSONS

Aberdeen, ART GALLERY AND IN-
DUSTRIAL MUSEUM: "Poplars in
a Thames Valley."

London, TATE GALLERY: "When
Nature Painted All Things
Gay."

PLATE 89

COTMAN

1850-1920

One of the Family

Walker Art Gallery, Liverpool

*

LATER BRITISH SCHOOL

*

FREDERICK COTMAN, nephew of the water-color painter, John Sell Cotman, was born at Ipswich, England, in 1850. A precocious talent with the crayon determined his career. Age of eighteen: Royal Academy Schools. Age of twenty: gold medal for distinction in historical painting. Then, a quiet, uneventful career in which he gained prominence as a painter of interiors and portraits. And prominence had its inevitable sequitur: election to the Royal Academy in 1882. Cotman exhibited extensively at international expositions, one of which—the Paris Fair of 1889—rewarded him with a silver medal. He submitted "One of the Family" to the Academy Exhibition of 1880. The painting was purchased subsequently for the Walker Art Gallery at Liverpool. Death came to him in 1920 at St. Ives, Huntingdonshire.

One of the Family

By COTMAN

"GO ANYWHERE in England where there are natural, whole-some, contented and really nice English people; and what do you always find? That the stables are the real center of the household."

—BERNARD SHAW, "Heartbreak House," Act Three.

PLATE 90

WHISTLER

1834-1903

The Little White Girl

National Gallery, London

✳

AMERICAN SCHOOL

✳

JAMES ABBOTT McNEILL WHISTLER, descended of Irish-American stock, was born at Lowell, Massachusetts, in 1834. In pursuance of the military tradition of his family, he was sent at the age of 17 to West Point. He was neither a good student nor by nature amenable to the discipline of an academy by whose system, it has been boasted, young men from all parts and classes of America, as different one from another as men can be, are turned out at graduation as alike as peas in a pod. After trying to enter the Navy, he was employed as draftsman in the Coast Survey. A number of his coast profile etchings are still to be found on the marine charts published by the department.

At the age of 20 he went to England and, a year later, to France. Here he was for two years a student in the atelier of the painter, Gleyre. Terming Gleyre a "bourgeois Greek," Whistler brought his academic studies to an end and entered [*Continued on plate 91*]

The Little White Girl

By WHISTLER

ART IS a means by which certain human beings convey to the rest of us their observations and impressions of life. Let the artist's intention be what it may, mankind will demand as a premise to the final and lasting acceptance of an art that it help man to a better understanding and appreciation of the world we live in and, through that, advance our happiness. And with all the authority of a jealous God we say to our fellows in regard to those "graven images" which are Art: "Thou shalt not bow down to *them,* nor worship *them.* Learn, rather, through your graven images to love *life* more." Yet it is the image *itself* that Whistler would have us love. We're wise unthinkingly, we people as a whole: we won't.

And yet here is this Little White Girl, so tenderly feminine that our hearts go out to her. Of a little girl in every way like her, we're moved to feel, Heine might have been thinking when he wrote:

> *Child, you are like a flower,*
> *So sweet and pure and fair;*
> *I look at you, and sadness*
> *Touches me with a prayer.*
>
> *I must lay my hands on your forehead*
> *And pray God to be sure*
> *To keep you forever and always*
> *So sweet and fair—and pure.*

From "Heinrich Heine, Paradox and Poet" by Louis Untermeyer. Copyright, 1937, by Harcourt, Brace and Company.

Softly, softly! Whistler must never know that we have come to love his little white girl far more than his art.

From the picture in the National Gallery, London
—by permission

PLATE 91

WHISTLER

1834-1903

Portrait of My Mother

Luxembourg, Paris

*

AMERICAN SCHOOL

*

[*Continued from plate 90*] with boundless confidence upon that career which was to lead through notoriety to honorable fame. Throughout his life, Whistler, by the independent character of his work and the sharpness of his tongue and pen, invited attack from the painters of the academic school and their apologists. Upon his failure of re-election at the age of 53 to the presidency of the Royal Society of British Artists he remarked that "The artists have come out and the British have remained."

Whistler's suit for damages against the critic, Ruskin, is a part of history, and has been devastatingly recorded by the brilliant pen of Whistler himself. A retort of Whistler's in the course of that trial is revealing of a kinship between Whistler's art principles and the name, at least, of the revolutionary movement which [*Continued on plate 92*]

Portrait of My Mother

By WHISTLER

THE NINETEENTH century saw all the Schools of European art merge and become that one debased and sterile thing, the Academic. Of the revolt against it Whistler is an example rather than a part. Related to the past, to Velasquez, to Vermeer (remotely), to the Japanese, his relatives were his own choosing. How much of the defiantly different behavior of one who is by nature different from his fellows is to be attributed to self-defense, how much of Whistler's cultivated enmity and the employment of witty sophistry for the annihilation of what he had cultivated is to be attributed to self-defense, is a question for psychologists. That Whistler's was a personality endowed with an inherent right and strength to live, his work attests. And of the extreme sensibility of his nature it is the lasting, touching evidence. Of his writings as expositions of his own believed philosophy, we must be critical. If he *believed* his published creed, he lived and worked beyond it. And if his "Arrangement in Gray and Black," had been, in fact, no more than that it would never, under the name which the world bestowed upon it, "Portrait of My Mother," have been so universally loved as it is.

From the picture in the Luxembourg, Paris

91

PLATE 92

WHISTLER

1834-1903

Portrait of Thomas Carlyle

Corporation Art Gallery, Glasgow

*

AMERICAN SCHOOL

*

[*Continued from plate 91*] was then approaching its height in France. The matter in question at the trial was the alleged obscure manner in which Whistler had painted a bridge at night. Whistler retorted by asking whether the artist was expected to visit the scene during the daytime and negotiate for its detail. Whistler was, in the literal sense of the term, an *Impressionist.*

In the newly discovered graphic medium, lithography, and the art of etching, Whistler's accomplishments are of great importance. And while his extensive influence as a painter was short-lived, his reputation as a master will endure. He died in London in 1903 at the age of 69.

Portrait of Thomas Carlyle

By WHISTLER

SO OBVIOUS, so insistent in all but every Whistler painting, is his preoccupation with line and pattern and the exquisite and subtle nuances of color harmony, that we may be forgiven for leaving them untalked about. That esthetics should have been the painter's chief concern is consistent with his own untenable creed that it is a grace which art bestows on nature. His often-quoted disparagement of sunsets embraced to Whistler the whole natural world and all the people in it. Whistler's attitude (or posture) towards everything that human beings, so long as they remain human, will love, is summed up by that most proper exponent of the whole precious school of thought, Oscar Wilde:

"Nobody of any real culture ever talks nowadays about the beauty of a sunset. Sunsets are quite old-fashioned. They belong to the time when Turner was the last note in art."

Whistler and Wilde are gone; and cultures come to be, to live a while, and die. And the sun rises: and people and all living things are made glad by it. And when it sets they're touched and saddened by its beauty. Life goes on.

Carlyle lives on; more, almost, in *spite* of Whistler's art he lives in Whistler's painting. We don't read Carlyle: he's too pompous. We wouldn't like him if we did; we are of a democracy. We read that he in life was difficult. Yes; but a kindly, somewhat weary, worn old man: Whistler has told us that.

From the picture in the Corporation Art Gallery, Glasgow
—by permission

Andover, Mass., PHILLIPS ACADEMY: "Old Battersea Bridge – Brown and Silver."

Baltimore, HATTON COLLECTION: "The Fish Wife."

Boston, MUSEUM OF FINE ARTS: "Portrait of Rose Whistler," "Little Rose of Lyme Regis."

Cambridge, FOGG ART MUSEUM: "Sunday Morning, Domberg."

Chicago, ART INSTITUTE: "Southampton Water," "Gray and Green – the Silver Sea," "Gray and Silver – Battersea Bridge," and others.

Cincinnati, ART MUSEUM: "Seascape."

Cincinnati, WILLIAMS COLLECTION: "Nocturne."

Cleveland, EELLS COLLECTION: "The Violin Player."

Cleveland, THE KING COLLECTION: "Street Scene, London Fog."

Detroit, INSTITUTE OF ART: "Self-Portrait," "Portrait of Robert Barr."

Detroit, THE PARKER COLLECTION: "Seascape."

Farmington, Conn., POPE-BROOKS FOUNDATION: "The Last of Old Westminster Bridge," "The Blue Wave."

Glasgow, CORPORATION ART GALLERY: "Portrait of Thomas Carlyle."

Hartford, WADSWORTH ATHENEUM: "The Coast of Brittany."

London, NATIONAL GALLERY: "The Little White Girl," "Cremorne Lights."

London, TATE GALLERY: "Nocturne in Blue and Gold – Old Battersea Bridge."

Naugatuck, Conn., WHITTEMORE COLLECTION: "The White Girl," "The Andalusian," "The Sea."

New Orleans, HENDERSON COLLECTION: "La Note Rouge," "La Belle du Jour," "Chelsea Fruit Shop," "Maud," "Maud Reading in a Hammock," and several portraits.

New York, FRICK COLLECTION: "The Ocean," "Portrait of Count Robert de Montesquiou-Fezensac," "Portrait of Rosa Corder," and other portraits.

New York, METROPOLITAN MUSEUM OF ART: "Cremorne Gardens, No. 2," "Connie Gilchrist Skipping."

New York, PRIVATE COLLECTIONS: Many examples, especially in the Hellman Collection.

Paris, LUXEMBOURG: "Portrait of My Mother."

Philadelphia, MUSEUM OF ART: "Portrait of Lady Archibald Campbell."

Philadelphia, PENNSYLVANIA MUSEUM OF ART: "Grand Canal, Venice – Moonlight."

Philadelphia, PRIVATE COLLECTIONS: Several examples.

St. Louis, WASHINGTON UNIVERSITY: "Nocturne in Blue and Silver."

Toledo, MUSEUM OF ART: "Crépuscule in Opal, Trouville."

Washington, FREER ART GALLERY: "Thames in Ice," "A Princess of the Land of Porcelain," "Annabel Lee," "The White Symphony – Three Girls," "Nocturne, Blue and Silver – Battersea Reach," and several others.

Washington, SMITHSONIAN INSTITUTION NATIONAL COLLECTION OF FINE ARTS: "Chelsea Embankment – Nocturne in Gray and Silver," "Chelsea – Rose and Gray," "Portrait of the Artist with a Hat," "The Frozen Thames."

Wellesley, Mass., FARNSWORTH MUSEUM: "The Neapolitan Girl – Rose and Gold."

Worcester, ART MUSEUM: "The Fur Jacket."

PLATE 93

WINSLOW HOMER

1836-1910

The Fox Hunt

Pennsylvania Academy of the Fine Arts, Philadelphia

*

AMERICAN SCHOOL

*

WINSLOW HOMER, descended of New England stock, was born in Boston on February 24, 1836. Homer's approach to a career in art was that of a young man looking for a means of livelihood. At the age of nineteen he was apprenticed to a lithographer. Two years later he established himself in a studio of his own in Boston and employed himself in making drawings for wood-cut reproduction.

Homer was in his middle twenties when the Civil War broke out. He joined the troops as an artist-reporter for *Harper's Weekly;* and much of his work, translated into woodcuts, is to be found in the *Weekly's* files of the period. Wartime events were the subjects of his earlier paintings. One of these, "Prisoners from the Front," is popular to this day. It was exhibited in New York in 1865, and two years later in Paris where he had in the meantime gone to study. That short period abroad furnished Homer his only academic training in art.

At the age of forty-eight he permanently left New York and established himself in that environment, the coast of Maine, which his subsequent great paintings of the sea show to have been so congenial to his nature. He died there in 1910 at the age of seventy-four.

The Fox Hunt

By WINSLOW HOMER

SO MUCH is made of "schools"—as though the term were of a definite, inclusive and exclusive significance comparable to the label of a geographical or governmental unit! "Winslow Homer: American School": how could he have been when there was then no American School? He is related in spirit to that nineteenth-century French revolutionary in realism, Gustave Courbet. To Manet—sometimes, superficially, by chance. His art, matured before he ever went abroad, was the natural unstrained outgrowth of his early work as illustrator. Homer the Realist: why realism was his *job* in youth! The actual, stark, unadorned reporting in pictures of those three-dimensional realities which his normal eyes encountered. Homer never sought to "express himself." He doubtless loathed the term. "Das Ding an sich"—the Thing Itself—he saw. He painted it. And without the least concern —so we may judge—as to whether what he did was art or wasn't, just simply loving what he did, he became the great and solitary master of realism that he is.

Strong, simple, honest, true, and by the power of those qualities profoundly moving, we claim him proudly as an exemplar of the American character. Maybe he is.

From the picture in the Pennsylvania Academy of the Fine Arts, Philadelphia
—by permission

Amherst, AMHERST COLLEGE: "The Fisher Girl."

Andover, PHILLIPS ACADEMY: "Boys in a Dory," "Eight Bells," "On the Cliff," "New England Country School," "West Wind."

Boston, MUSEUM OF FINE ARTS: "The Lookout," "The Fog Warning," "Dory," "Fishing Boats, Devonshire," "Montagnais Indians, Pointe Bleue, Quebec," "The Fallen Deer," "Landscape."

Brooklyn, MUSEUM: "Bear and Canoe," "The Turtle Pound," "The Unruly Calf," "Shooting the Rapids," "In the White Mountains," "Key West," and others.

Cambridge, FOGG ART MUSEUM: "Negro under Palm," "Fishing in the Adirondacks," "Canoe in Rapids."

Chicago, ART INSTITUTE: "Camp Fire, Adirondacks," "Marblehead," "Adirondack Guide," "The Herring Net," "Coast of Maine," and others.

Cincinnati, ART MUSEUM: "Hauling in Anchor," "A Sunday Morning in Virginia."

Cleveland, THE KING COLLECTION: "Leaping Trout."

Cleveland, MUSEUM OF ART: "Early Morning after a Storm at Sea."

Detroit, THE INSTITUTE OF ARTS: "Bahama Boatman," "Prout's Neck."

Hartford, WADSWORTH ATHENEUM: "A Moonlight Sea."

Lawrence, Kansas, THAYER MUSEUM OF ART: "Cloud Shadows."

Minneapolis, INSTITUTE OF ART: "The Conch Divers."

New York, AMERICAN ACADEMY OF ARTS AND LETTERS: "The Incoming Tide."

New York, COOPER UNION MUSEUM: "The Yellow Jacket," "Gathering Autumn Leaves," and others.

New York, METROPOLITAN MUSEUM OF ART: "Prisoners from the Front," "Camp Fire," "The Carnival," "Gulf Stream," "Searchlight, Harbor Entrance, Santiago de Cuba," "Harvest," "Cannon Rock," "Bermuda," "Maine Coast," "Northeaster," "High Tide," "Moonlight, Woods Island Light," "Fishing Boats, Key West."

New York, PRIVATE COLLECTIONS: Many examples.

Northampton, SMITH COLLEGE MUSEUM: "The Song of the Lark."

Philadelphia, MUSEUM OF ART: "The Life Line," "Huntsman and Dogs."

Philadelphia, PENNSYLVANIA ACADEMY OF THE FINE ARTS: "The Fox Hunt."

Pittsburgh, CARNEGIE INSTITUTE: "The Wreck."

Princeton, UNIVERSITY MUSEUM: "The Fan."

Providence, RHODE ISLAND SCHOOL OF DESIGN: "Girl and Daisies," "Fishing," "Boy and Horse," and others.

San Diego, FINE ARTS GALLERY: "Portrait of Captain Smith."

Toledo, MUSEUM OF FINE ARTS: "Sunlight on the Coast."

Washington, CORCORAN GALLERY: "A Light on the Sea."

Washington, FREER ART GALLERY: "Waterfall in the Adirondacks."

Washington, PHILLIPS MEMORIAL GALLERY: "To the Rescue," "On the Cliffs."

Washington, UNITED STATES NATIONAL GALLERY OF ART: "A Visit from Old Mistress," "High Cliff, Coast of Maine."

Worcester, ART MUSEUM: "Boys and Kitten," "In a Florida Jungle," "Old Friend," "Lake St. John," and many others.

Youngstown, BUTLER ART INSTITUTE: "Snap the Whip."

PLATE 94

THOMAS EAKINS

1844-1916

The Thinker

Metropolitan Museum of Art, New York

*

AMERICAN SCHOOL

*

THOMAS EAKINS was born in Philadelphia in 1844. It was the happy belief of artists in that day that art, a trade quite unrelated to its time and native place, was to be learned abroad and practised here. We recall that Calvin Coolidge at so late a date as his incumbency of the White House saw no need for the cultivation of art in America. "Couldn't we," he asked, "get all the art we want from France?" And the belief that men could *best* study art in France or Munich was tacitly accepted in America until the beginning of this century. So Eakins, voyaging to France, submitted his talents to the discipline of the École des Beaux-Arts and its great master of the day, Gérôme. Eakins survived; and if French influence is to be found in his subsequent work it is rather that of the painter, Bonnet, with whom he studied later.

Eakins, while in Paris, studied for a while with the sculptor, Dumont. It may be that to that study is to be attributed the sculptural quality noticeable in his later work. We incline rather to believe that it was an expression of Eakins' own feeling for form, itself the cause rather than the effect of his having studied sculpture. Eakins, after his return to Philadelphia, was for some years a teacher of anatomy in the Pennsylvania Academy of Fine Arts in Philadelphia. He died in Philadelphia in 1916.

The Thinker

By EAKINS

THOMAS EAKINS has been termed "a painter's painter." This is a tribute to his mastery of those technical problems in painting which are basic to the craft, and an assertion, implied, that few outside the craft will like his work. Let us, at any rate, concede his mastery.

Basic to "realism" is the representation of form—men, mountains, tree trunks, tables, *things*—as having volume, weight, and substance. To the two-dimensional plane of the canvas must be added the illusion of that third dimension which all matter has. We term it what the Bible calls it, form.

> And the earth was without form, and void; and darkness was upon the face of the deep. And God said, "Let there be light": and there was light.

And by that light, day after day, did form reveal itself. So does the master-painter, out of the chaos and darkness of his pigments, create the illusion of a world. And of these master-painters, Eakins was one.

What, having made his figures live and move and have their being, Eakins does with them is another matter and probably at the root of the continued popular neglect of his work. And yet it may be that posterity will find the factual commonplaceness of his people to be an added reason to respect and love his paintings.

From the picture in the Metropolitan Museum of Art, New York
—by permission

94

PRINCIPAL WORKS BY EAKINS

Andover, PHILLIPS ACADEMY: "Salutat," "Portrait of Professor Rowland," "Elisabeth at the Piano."

Boston, MUSEUM OF FINE ARTS: "Starting Out After Rail."

Brooklyn, MUSEUM OF ART: "Whistling for Plover," "Portrait of Letitia Wilson Jordan Bacon."

Chicago, ART INSTITUTE: "Music."

Cleveland, MUSEUM OF ART: "The Biglen Brothers Turning the Stake Boat."

Detroit, INSTITUTE OF ART: "Portrait of Dr. Horatio C. Wood," "Portrait of Robert M. Lindsay," "Portrait of A. B. Frost."

Fort Worth, MUSEUM OF ART: "The Swimming Hole."

New Haven, YALE UNIVERSITY GALLERY OF FINE ARTS: "Taking the Count."

New York, AMERICAN SCENIC AND HISTORIC PRESERVATION SOCIETY: "Portrait of Rutherford B. Hayes."

New York, METROPOLITAN MUSEUM OF ART: "Max Schmitt in a Single Scull," "John Biglen in in a Single Scull," "Chess Players," "The Thinker," "The Writing Master," "Portrait of a Lady with a Setter Dog."

New York, NATIONAL ACADEMY OF DESIGN: "The Wrestlers," "Self-Portrait."

Philadelphia, JEFFERSON MEDICAL COLLEGE: "The Surgical Clinic of Professor Gross," "Portrait of Professor Benjamin H. Rand."

Philadelphia, MUSEUM OF ART: "Mending the Net," "Oarsmen," "Taking up the Net," "Between the Rounds," "The Black Fan," "Addie."

Philadelphia, PENNSYLVANIA ACADEMY OF THE FINE ARTS: "The Cello Player."

Washington, CORCORAN GALLERY OF ART: "The Pathetic Song."

Washington, PHILLIPS MEMORIAL GALLERY: "Portrait of Miss Van Buren."

PLATE 95

FRANCIS DAVIS MILLET

1846-1912

Between Two Fires

Tate Gallery, London

*

AMERICAN SCHOOL

*

FRANCIS DAVIS MILLET was born at Mattapoisette, Massachusetts, 1842. His first occupation, as drummer-boy in the Massachusetts Volunteers during the Civil War, was the consistent beginning of a strenuous career. He graduated from Harvard in 1869 and traveled to Antwerp to study painting. The Russo-Turkish War began during one of his visits to England. Millet covered the battlefronts for the London *Daily News*. Twenty years later he repeated this excursion into journalism by serving as reporter for the London *Times* at Manila during the Spanish-American War. His willingness to assume additional burdens brought him many official duties. He was Director of Decorations at the Columbian Exposition in 1893, trustee of the Metropolitan Museum in New York, secretary of the American Academy at Rome, and delegate to many foreign international expositions. With all his travels and public services, Millet found time to translate Tolstoi and write several books of travel, essays, and short stories. His work in painting was chiefly decorative and may be seen in Trinity Church, Boston; The Capitol, St. Paul; and the Bank of Pittsburgh.

Millet went down with the *Titanic* in 1912.

Between Two Fires

By FRANCIS DAVIS MILLET

A PURITAN gentleman, austere and humorless, wants nothing more than to say his grace alone. But a public inn is sparing of its privacy. Two bold maids, having served his meal, refuse to serve his soul. They tease this pious visitor, waiting for his anger to mount, hoping that his restraint will give way to an untempered oath and a violent command to leave the room. The Puritan sits tight upon his spleen and tries violently to control his growing indignation.

Here the scenario stops. Fill in the climax. It's half the fun of story-telling pictures.

From the picture in the Tate Gallery, London
—by permission

95

PRINCIPAL WORKS BY MILLET

Baltimore, UNITED STATES CUSTOMS HOUSE: "The Evolution of Navigation."

Cleveland, THE CLEVELAND TRUST COMPANY: "The Puritans," "Father Hennepin at Niagara," "Trader and an Indian in a Canoe."

Detroit, INSTITUTE OF ART: "Reading the Story of Oenone."

Hannibal, Mo., LIBRARY: "Portrait of Mark Twain."

London, TATE GALLERY: "Between Two Fires."

Montreal, GALLERY: "The Tired Guard."

Newark, ESSEX COUNTY COURT HOUSE: "Rebuking the Chief Justice."

New York, METROPOLITAN MUSEUM OF ART: "A Cozy Corner," "An Old-Time Melody."

New York, UNION LEAGUE CLUB: "At the Inn."

PLATE 96

ALBERT RYDER

1847-1917

The Race Track

Cleveland Museum of Art

*

AMERICAN SCHOOL

*

ALBERT PINKHAM RYDER was born at New Bedford, Massachusetts, on March 18, 1847. He became a pupil in New York of William Marshall and of the school of The National Academy of Design, the latter an influence in its day as repressive of natural self-expression and young talent as any that he could have encountered. But Ryder was perhaps no more inclined by nature to explore new methods of expression than to find in accepted methods anything to limit him in what he chose to express. His style was of a dozen schools: he was of none of them. Nor was he of that little world of New York in which he lived. Retiring to the seclusion which a busy city offers, he worked alone, in utter disregard of the immediate world about him and neglect of his material life. The recognition that came to him was small but, for his small needs, ample. And although his methods of work were painstakingly slow, years being spent on single works, his sales to wealthy patrons yielded him sufficient for his simple wants.

He died at Elmhurst, Long Island, on March 28, 1917. And in 1918 the Metropolitan Museum in New York held that memorial exhibition of his works which proclaimed to the whole world the greatness of his genius.

The Race Track

By ALBERT RYDER

RYDER is listed as of the American School: he is no more of the American School than of the School of Barbizon or Flanders, Venice, Greece or Rome. He suggests Monticelli: what of it? And Blake, his Vergil wood-cuts: did he know Blake? Who knows! And Wagner by his subjects. And Shakespeare. And the Old Testament, and the New. Is it that by suggesting so many influences he invites our cataloguing them? Or that so few, or none at all, being there, we are driven to the ends of the world and history to seek for clues? Why is it, after all, that Ryder stirs us so? Is it his art as art, or, through his art, himself? How can it be himself when he, the man, is as remote and undefined a presence in his work as back-stage Shakespeare?

It is not Ryder, nor his dusty molten-jewel quality of paint, nor the arrangement of his light and shadow. Hardly is it, we are made to feel, his art. From before the unearthly, tragic world of the unconscious, of the unconscious of us all, of all time, everywhere, of the underworld Aeneas visited, Ryder, who in the solitude of a New York tenement had found that world and come to live in it, draws back the curtain.

From the picture in the Cleveland Museum of Art
—by permission

PRINCIPAL WORKS BY RYDER

Andover, PHILLIPS ACADEMY: "Constance," "Toilers of the Sea," "Way of the Cross."

Buffalo, FINE ARTS ACADEMY: "Temple of the Mind."

Cambridge, FOGG ART MUSEUM: "White Horse."

Chicago, CUDNEY COLLECTION: "Elegy in a Country Churchyard," "Diana's Hunt."

Cleveland, MUSEUM OF ART: "The Race Track," ("Death on a Pale Horse").

Denver, ART MUSEUM: "Moonlit Sail."

Detroit, INSTITUTE OF ARTS: "Early Morning," "Moonlight Scene."

Minneapolis, INSTITUTE OF ARTS: "Return of the Peasant."

New York, METROPOLITAN MUSEUM OF ART: "Nourmahal," "Autumn Meadows."

Providence, RHODE ISLAND SCHOOL OF DESIGN: "Sailing by Moonlight."

Washington, PHILLIPS MEMORIAL GALLERY: "The Resurrection," "Macbeth and the Witches," "Moonlit Cove," "Gay Head," "The Dead Bird."

Worcester, ART MUSEUM: "Pegasus."

PLATE 97

JOHN SINGER SARGENT

1856-1925

Carnation, Lily, Lily, Rose

Tate Gallery, London

*

AMERICAN SCHOOL

*

AMONG THE first generation of the settlers of Gloucester, Massachusetts, was the Sargent family of Gloucester, England. And in Gloucester, Massachusetts, Dr. Fitzwilliam Sargent, the father of John Singer Sargent, was born. He married, in due time, Mary Newbold Singer, of an old Philadelphia family. With little thought of making Europe their residence, the young couple in 1854 went abroad. And two years later, in Florence, their son, John Singer Sargent, was born.

His talent showed itself in early youth and was encouraged by his mother whose own pastime it was to sketch in water-colors. At the Accademia in Florence he won a prize for drawing at the age of seventeen. At eighteen he was a student in the studio of Carolus Duran in Paris; and from Duran, whose own work was based upon a study of Frans Hals and Velasquez, Sargent acquired much that was to characterize his work throughout his life. Sargent's success as a painter was immediate. Writing in 1881, Henry James said, "It is a talent which on the very threshold of its career has nothing more to learn."

In the Salon of 1884—Sargent was then twenty-eight years old—was exhibited a portrait of Madame Gautreau which, by the storm that was raised by the [*Continued on plate 98*]

Carnation, Lily, Lily, Rose

By SARGENT

SARGENT had eyes; he saw. And what he saw he painted with the fluent ease of one whose mind was untroubled by questions. What life appeared to be, it was. No more. One summer's evening he saw lighted Chinese lanterns hanging in a garden of lilies. Twilight, white flowers, and the lantern glow: it was so lovely that he wanted to paint a picture of it. And so he arranged a comparable scene in the flower garden of a friend; and his friend's two little daughters put on white dresses and posed as though lighting the lanterns. The white of their dresses matched the white of the lilies; the red of their lips, the carnations and roses. It was a pretty scene. Well, here in Sargent's picture it is, just as he saw it. He named the picture "Carnation, Lily, Lily, Rose" from a line in a song of the season.

Whistler, who cultivated what he called "The Gentle Art of Making Enemies," didn't like such things. He called the picture, "Damnation, Silly, Silly Pose."

From the picture in the Tate Gallery, London
—by permission

Andover, Mass., PHILLIPS ACADEMY: "Val d'Aosta — Man Fishing," "Cypress Trees at San Vigilio."

Baltimore, JOHNS HOPKINS UNIVERSITY MUSEUM: "Portrait of Mary Elizabeth Garrett."

Boston, GARDNER COLLECTION: "Portrait of Mrs. Isabella Stuart Gardner" (two versions), "The Bridge, Venice," and many others.

Boston, MUSEUM OF FINE ARTS: "Corfu — Lights and Shadows," "Daphne," "La Blancheria," a series of mythological and allegorical murals, and many other easel paintings.

Boston, PRIVATE COLLECTIONS: Many examples.

Boston, PUBLIC LIBRARY: "The History of Religion," a mural series.

Boston, SARGENT ESTATE: "Palm Thicket," "Landing, Miami," "Negro Drinking," and others.

Boston, SUPREME COURT BUILDING: "Portrait of William Caleb Loring."

Brooklyn, INSTITUTE: "Venetian Boats," "La Riva degli Schiavoni," and others, constituting probably the most numerous Sargent collection in America.

Brooklyn, MUSEUM: "Portrait of A. Augustus Healy."

Bryn Mawr, COLLEGE: "Portrait of Miss M. Carey Thomas."

Buffalo, FINE ARTS ACADEMY: "Venetian Bead Stringers," "Portrait of Elsie Palmer."

Cambridge, FOGG ART MUSEUM: "Lake O'Hara," "The Brook," "The Glaciers," "Camping near Lake O'Hara."

Cambridge, HARVARD UNIVERSITY: "Portrait of Abbott Lawrence Lowell," "Portrait of Charles William Eliot," "Portrait of Henry Lee Higginson."

Cambridge, PRIVATE COLLECTIONS: Several examples.

Cambridge, WIDENER LIBRARY: "The American Soldiers Arrive," "Victory and Death."

Chicago, ART INSTITUTE: "The Weavers," "The Fountain," "Venetian Glass Workers," and several portraits.

Chicago, PRIVATE COLLECTIONS: Many examples.

Cincinnati, MUSEUM ASSOCIATION: "Two Girls Fishing."

Cincinnati, PRIVATE COLLECTIONS: Many examples.

Cincinnati, TAFT COLLECTION INSTITUTE OF FINE ARTS: "Portrait of Robert Louis Stevenson."

Cleveland, MUSEUM OF ART: "The Cossack."

Danvers, Mass., ENDICOTT COLLECTION: "Portrait of William Crowninshield Endicott, Jr.," and other portraits.

Detroit, INSTITUTE OF ARTS: "Home Fields."

Dover, Mass., HALE COLLECTION: "Magnolias," "Schooner *Catherine*," "A Sandy Beach."

Groton, Mass., PEABODY COLLECTION: "Portrait of the Rev. Endicott Peabody."

Haverhill, Mass., WEBSTER COLLECTION: "By the Brook."

Indianapolis, JOHN HERRON ART INSTITUTE: "Portrait of James Whitcomb Riley."

London, NATIONAL PORTRAIT GALLERY: "Portrait of Coventry Patmore."

London, TATE GALLERY: "Portrait of Lord Ribblesdale," "Portrait of Mrs. Wertheimer," "Carnation, Lily, Lily, Rose," and others.

Madison, Wisconsin, STATE HISTORICAL SOCIETY: "Portrait of General Lucius Fairchild."

(*Continued*)

PLATE 98

JOHN SINGER SARGENT

1856-1925

Lord Ribblesdale

Tate Gallery, London

*

AMERICAN SCHOOL

*

[*Continued from plate 97*] lady's political friends and sustained by the critics of the French press, brought Sargent world-wide notoriety. Once started, the hounds of the press were persistent in their outcry; and Sargent, thoroughly and finally disgusted with critics, left Paris and moved to London. His residence in London was unbroken throughout his life but for occasional visits to the continent and to America.

He had been described as "a tall commanding presence, with a small head well set on broad shoulders, with large, somewhat prominent gray eyes, kindly in expression. . . . During the last years of his life, with his great size, his dark hair and beard turned silver white, his florid complexion, and an air about him of singular freshness and calm, he had a look of some serene and benevolent Jove." Both as artist and man he was a commanding personality for forty years before his death. Sargent himself dismissed the claims of rhapsodists that he showed himself in his work to be a psychologist and a satirist. "I chronicle," he once said. "I do not judge."

John Sargent died in 1925. Memorial services were held at Westminster Abbey; and a replica in bronze of his "Crucifixion" in the Boston Library has been placed in the crypt of St. Paul's Cathedral.

Lord Ribblesdale

By SARGENT

TITIAN and Tintoretto, Van Dyck, Reynolds and Gainsborough; Romney, Raeburn, Lawrence: if we could only set these names in diminishing type like the Mouse's tail in "Alice in Wonderland"! Down, down in size as we ascend the years, as dignity yields to sentiment, sentiment to mawkishness, all to be swept aside by that most Spencerian balderdash of brush strokes which commemorates the looks and brains of fashionable charm and manhood at the nineteenth century's close. And at the end of the tail, just where it tapers out, a nubbin, button, tassel, ornament: John Sargent. And if we Americans may claim as ours and one of our "school" a man who lived his life abroad and who, even if there had been an American School in his time, was, as a painter, English to the core, then let us take John Sargent to our hearts. For at his best he was the most distinguished exponent of modern times of a great school of portraiture.

Lord Ribblesdale: A life-long Liberal, a sportsman, a friend of Britain's monarchs—Victoria, Edward VII, George V. He died in 1925.

*From the picture in the Tate Gallery, London
—by permission*

Miami, DEERING ESTATE: "Three Boats in the Harbor of San Vigilio, Lake Garda," "Portrait of Mme. Paul Escudier," "Portrait of Hercules Brabazon Brabazon."

Minneapolis, INSTITUTE OF ARTS: "Portrait of Mrs. Thomas Lincoln Manson," "The Luxembourg Gardens at Night."

New York, HISPANIC SOCIETY: "Spanish Dance."

New York, METROPOLITAN MUSEUM OF ART: "Gitana," "Marble Quarry at Carrara," "Portrait of Mme. X (Mme. Gautreau)," "Tyrolese Interior," and several others.

New York, NATIONAL ACADEMY OF DESIGN: "Self-Portrait," "Portrait of Claude Monet."

New York, PLAYERS CLUB: "Portrait of Joseph Jefferson," "Portrait of Edwin Booth," "Portrait of Lawrence Barrett."

New York, PRIVATE COLLECTIONS AND SALES GALLERIES: Many pieces.

Paris, LUXEMBOURG: "Carmencita."

Philadelphia, MUSEUM OF ART: "Portrait of Lady Eden," "The Rialto," "Portrait of the Duchess of Sutherland."

Philadelphia, MUTUAL INSURANCE CO.: "Portrait of Dr. Silas Weir Mitchell."

Philadelphia, PENNSYLVANIA ACADEMY: "Portrait of Mr. and Mrs. J. W. Field."

Philadelphia, PRIVATE COLLECTIONS: Many examples.

Philadelphia, UNIVERSITY OF PENNSYLVANIA: "Portrait of Dr. James William White."

Pittsburgh, CARNEGIE INSTITUTE: "Venetian Interior."

Providence, RHODE ISLAND SCHOOL OF DESIGN: "Portrait of Manuel Garcia," "Portrait of Frederick Porter Vinton."

San Francisco, COWELL COLLECTION: "Trout Stream in the Tyrol."

Silver Spring, Md., McCORMICK-GOODHART COLLECTION: "The Forest Pool."

Toledo, MUSEUM OF ART: "Portrait of Princess Demidoff."

Trenton, MOON COLLECTION: "Canal in Venice."

Washington, CAPITOL BUILDING: "Portrait of Senator Thomas Brackett Reed."

Washington, CORCORAN GALLERY: "En Route pour la Pêche," "Oyster Gatherers at Cancale," "Portrait of Daniel J. Nolan."

Washington, FREER ART GALLERY: "The Weavers," "Breakfast in the Loggia," "Landscape with Goats."

Washington, PRIVATE COLLECTIONS: Several examples.

Washington, SMITHSONIAN INSTITUTION NATIONAL COLLECTION OF FINE ARTS: "Portrait of Betty Wertheimer."

Washington, WHITE HOUSE: "Portrait of Theodore Roosevelt."

Wilmington, DU PONT COLLECTION: "The Sphinx," "Villa Marlia, Lucca."

Worcester, ART MUSEUM: "The Patio – Vizcaya," "Boats at Anchor," "Palms," "The Bathers," "Venetian Water Carriers," and others.

PLATE 99

GEORGE BELLOWS

1882-1925

Portrait of the Artist's Mother

Art Institute of Chicago

*

AMERICAN SCHOOL

*

GEORGE WESLEY BELLOWS was born in Columbus, Ohio, in 1882. His interest in art which had grown throughout his college years had so matured at the time of his graduation in 1904 that, having chosen art as his vocation, he moved to New York and took up the study of it under Robert Henri. He was a brilliant student; and the dramatic vitality and near sensationalism of his first exhibited work attracted early attention. The vitality of his work was consistent with his own nature. He was physically strong, a superb ball player, and a natural leader, through his personal qualities as well as through his accomplishment, of the important young movement in American art into which he was born and which he was so forcefully to promote. He married a gifted and beautiful fellow-student, Emma Story, and the happiness of their life together is reflected in his many portraits of the family. At the age of 43, at the very height of his powers and his fame, George Bellows was stricken by appendicitis and died.

Portrait of the Artist's Mother

By GEORGE BELLOWS

OF FEW painters can it be said with assurance: His work is the complete expression of himself. We say it of George Bellows. Whatever in the art of Bellows is derived (and all art has its derivations) he had absorbed unthinkingly from those art influences of the past and of his time which were current in the New York of his student days. What in its truest sense is any culture but the transmutation into a single cultural entity of the many and heterogeneous elements that circumstances have brought together? Such is that Melting Pot, America. And of America, of its Middle West and New York, of its schools and ball fields, of its cities, soil, air, light and darkness, Life, is Bellows. And what he is, even what he lacked, his work proclaims. His paintings and lithographs have the force and energy that we proudly believe to be American. What we believe, we are—or will become. And in his pictures' faults, their brashness and occasional insensibility, we'll read our common faults and, reading, profit.

From the picture in the Art Institute of Chicago
—by permission

PRINCIPAL WORKS BY GEORGE BELLOWS

Andover, PHILLIPS ACADEMY: "Outside the Big Tent."

Boston, MUSEUM OF FINE ARTS: "Emma and Her Children."

Brooklyn, MUSEUM: "The Sand Team."

Buffalo, FINE ARTS ACADEMY: "Elinor, Jean, and Anna."

Chicago, ART INSTITUTE: "Portrait of the Artist's Mother," "Love of Winter."

Cincinnati, MUSEUM ASSOCIATION: "Dawn of Peace," "Hail to Peace."

Cleveland, MUSEUM OF ART: "Boy," "Sharkey's."

Columbus, GALLERY OF FINE ARTS: "Portrait of the Artist's Mother," "Polo Game."

Columbus, OHIO STATE UNIVERSITY: "Portrait of Dr. Scott."

Des Moines, CARPENTER COLLECTION: "Aunt Fanny."

Detroit, INSTITUTE OF ARTS: "A Day in June."

Indianapolis, HERRON ART INSTITUTE: "A Boy."

Los Angeles, MUSEUM: "Cliff Dwellers."

Lynchburg, RANDOLPH-MACON COLLEGE: "Men of the Docks."

Newark, MUSEUM ASSOCIATION: "Three Pigs and a Mountain."

New York, METROPOLITAN MUSEUM OF ART: "Up the Hudson."

New York, WHITNEY MUSEUM: "Dempsey-Firpo."

Philadelphia, PENNSYLVANIA ACADEMY OF THE FINE ARTS: "North River."

Pittsburgh, CARNEGIE INSTITUTE: "Anne in White."

Pride's Crossing, Massachusetts, FRICK COLLECTION: "Ducks in Winter."

Providence, RHODE ISLAND SCHOOL OF DESIGN: "Rain on the River."

Savannah, THE TELFAIR ACADEMY: "Snow-capped River."

Toledo, MUSEUM: "The Bridge, Blackwell's Island."

Washington, CORCORAN GALLERY: "Forty-two Kids."

Washington, PHILLIPS' MEMORIAL GALLERY: "Emma at the Window."

Worcester, ART MUSEUM: "The White Horse."

A vast number of Bellow's works is in private collections and Mrs. Bellows at this writing still retains many pieces.

PLATE 100

GRANT WOOD

BORN 1892

Fall Plowing

Marshall Field Collection, New York

*

AMERICAN SCHOOL

*

THAT ART SHOULD be of a nature and character indigenous to the soil and culture out of which it has come into being is beyond controversy. It is our wishful belief that —taking for example the life of the American farmer—farm life, the lives of farmers and laborers, and of the women of the farm, can best be painted by themselves. This ought to be: it rarely is.

Grant Wood is an exception. He was born of Quaker stock on a small farm in Iowa in 1892. His father died when Grant was but 10 years old. Necessity forced work, hard work, upon the family; and the kid, Grant, earned what he could at every kind of manual work that came to hand. At night he drew, because he liked to. He was persistent. The war came and he fought in it. Anthrax got him down; he kept on drawing. After seven years as art teacher in Grand Rapids he went to France to study art. And when at last he got back home to Iowa, he learned.

Grant Wood, a recognized master of the American school of painting, should have this motto, framed in faked rustic with the corners crossed, hung on the wall of his bed-room: "Be it ever so humble, for art there is no place like home." Maybe just such a motto does hang there. At any rate, his work proclaims it.

Fall Plowing

By GRANT WOOD

GRANT WOOD of Iowa, American: He is to be classed as of one of the innumerable "American schools" which, under the sponsorship of our Federal government, notably the Art Projects of W.P.A., have sprung into being. Regional art, it is termed: being by its nature expressive of the life and landscape of the diverse regions of our North American continent. The decentralization of art, the demobilization of artists and students of art from such centers as New York, Philadelphia, and Chicago to which in past decades they had been drawn, and the financial encouragement—scant enough at its best!—which, first inviting artists to come home, has kept them there, has been the direct cause of that phenomenon of today which has been termed our Renaissance. It is, in fact, a birth. America, for three centuries a frontier of the cultural motherland, Europe; bound to it by tradition supported by the self interest of dealers in culture and the brainless subservience of Academies—America, at last, is free. Free to respect itself: our art proclaims it.

Of those to whom the American scene—its "rocks and rills," its "woods and templed hills," its fields of corn, alfalfa, cotton, wheat, potatoes, its barns and silos, its cities and industrial centers, its people and its life, America—is beautiful, Grant Wood is one. Like him or not, he's ours. God bless America!

From the picture in the Marshall Field Collection, New York
—by permission of the artist and by courtesy of Mr. Field

100

PRINCIPAL WORKS BY GRANT WOOD

Beverly Hills, California, EDWARD G. ROBINSON COLLECTION: "Daughters of Revolution."

Cedar Rapids, ART ASSOCIATION: "Portrait of Mrs. Francis Merryville Wood" ("Woman With Plants").

Cedar Rapids, THE WOODROW WILSON HIGH SCHOOL: "Young Corn."

Chicago, ART INSTITUTE: "American Gothic."

Des Moines, GARDNER COWLES, JR., COLLECTION: "Birthplace of Herbert Hoover."

Memphis, MRS. C. M. GOOCH COLLECTION: "Midnight Ride of Paul Revere."

New York, S. C. CLARK COLLECTION: "Dinner for Threshers."

New York, EDWIN HEWITT COLLECTION: "Arbor Day."

New York, MARSHALL FIELD COLLECTION: "Fall Plowing."

ALPHABETICAL INDEX OF PICTURES

References are to Plate Numbers. When a portrait is known by the name of its sitter, it is listed under that name.

ALPHABETICAL INDEX OF PAINTERS

References are to Plate Numbers.